⁓ The Bedroom ⁓

The Bedroom

Diane Berger

Photographs by

Fritz von der Schulenburg

Abbeville Press • Publishers • New York • Paris • London

*To my husband, Tom, for sharing my love of travel (the places we've visited together have inspired
many of the ideas in this book), and for his enthusiastic support throughout the project.*

*"To accommodate their Majesties with a good Bed, I made interest with Mr. Hill, Mr. Beckford's Steward,
to lend us his superb State Bed, which we brought to Wilton, slung on the Carriage of a Waggon, . . . at no small
expense, but what signifies money, when we were to entertain the Princes of the Land. . . . lo, and behold!
when they arrived, they brought a small double Tent Bed, had it put up in the Colonade Room, where the
State Bed was already placed, in a crack, and slept, for any thing I know to the contrary, quiet and well."*
*—Description of a visit by King George III to Wilton, 1778,
quoted by Mark Girouard in* A Country House Companion.

*Whether you long for a bed fit for a king or a folding tent bed,
this book is dedicated to helping you create the bedroom of your dreams.*

EDITOR: Jacqueline Decter
DESIGNER: Molly Shields
PRODUCTION EDITOR: Abigail Asher
PRODUCTION MANAGER: Lou Bilka

Caption information and attributions by Karen Howes, The Interior World.

First edition
10 9 8 7 6 5 4 3 2 1

Photography Credits
PAGE 10: Royal Academy of Arts Library, © reserved Royal Academy of Arts.
PAGE 11: British Architectural Library, RIBA, London. © Royal Institute of British
Architects. Photography and processing by A. C. Cooper Ltd.
PAGE 14: Collection, Stefanie Maison. Photography by Prudence Cuming Associates, Ltd.

Library of Congress Cataloging-in-Publication Data
Berger, Diane (Diane L.)
    The bedroom / Diane Berger ; photographs by Fritz von der
Schulenburg.
        p.   cm.
    Includes bibliographical references and index.
    ISBN 1-55859-799-9 (acid-free paper)
    1. Bedrooms.   2. Bedroom furniture.   3. Interior decoration.
I. Von der Schulenburg, Fritz.   II. Title.
NK2117.B4B4   1995
747.787—dc20   95-11780

CONTENTS

INTRODUCTION

As the most private, intimate space in the house, the bedroom is endowed with a special aura. It offers us the promise of relaxation, romance, passion, and inner peace. It nurtures tired body and soul by cocooning us in serenity and comfort, and it seduces us with the anticipation of entering soothing dream states that magically transport us away from the workaday world, if only for a few precious hours. But our dreams need not be confined to sleep. The very privacy of the bedroom allows us the decorative freedom to transform our dreams into visual reality, giving expression to our innermost selves. There are as many ways to decorate the bedroom as there are dreamers, and whether your vision of the ideal bedroom is a simple mattress placed directly on the floor in a pristine white room or a luscious "wilderness of faded chintz," in the words of Henry James, the following pages are filled with irresistible ideas that will help you to create the bedroom of your dreams.

"Houses, like all other architecture, are images of the society that built them. Throughout the centuries, they have altered as much with custom as with fashion," historian James Chambers has written. Much the same can be said of the bedroom. From Saxon times through the Middle Ages, the bed-

room as we know it today did not exist. Most people, with the exception of the very wealthy, lived in dwellings consisting of a single hall-like space that played host to all of life's domestic activities, including eating, sleeping, entertaining, lovemaking, and even sheltering animals. This one-room house endured in some places into the seventeenth century, except among the elite. As people accumulated wealth and became more landed, they also became more status-conscious. Desiring to distance themselves from the hurly-burly of the hall, high-ranking individuals began to build separate rooms off the hall where they could sleep apart from the other members of their extended households. The creation of a private space specifically for sleeping served to differentiate this daily activity from the rest and to imbue the room itself with importance. The privacy it afforded, however, made it an ideal place not only for sleeping but also for intimate dining and for holding confidential audiences. Thus, these early bedrooms had a multipurpose, semi-public function.

By the eighteenth century, in both England and France, aristocratic and royal dwellings, although differently organized, typically featured a bedroom preceded by a series of rooms and sometimes adjoined by an even more intimate closet to which one fled when the bedroom became too public. The need for guests to approach the bedroom through an avenue of increasingly private rooms, or "axis of honour," as historian Mark Girouard describes it, was clear evidence of social standing. When English diarist Mary Berry was fortunate enough to gain access to Josephine Bonaparte's private apartments in 1802, she noted that "permission [was] obtained only by favour as it is by no means shown to all the world." Palaces and aristocratic houses where royal guests were likely to visit had sumptuously decorated bedrooms of state that were intended to dazzle through sheer opulence and were reserved almost exclusively for ceremonial purposes, showing to what extent the notion of the bedroom as an indicator of status had become entrenched in the social fabric. Louis XIV had already made the institution of the levée—the practice of receiving royal visitors while attending to his morning toilette—infamous. This tradition filtered down through the ranks of a beau monde eager to imitate aristocratic customs.

The advent of Romanticism ushered in a more relaxed attitude toward rigid class distinctions. This more democratic spirit signaled the end of the bedroom's heyday as a reception room. Shifting tides of fashion swept in a vogue for grand-scale socializing in the form of balls, assemblies, and tea parties, which necessitated the creation of big public reception rooms to accommodate large numbers of guests. As a result, the bedroom gradually retreated into the recesses of private life, where it has remained ever since. The changing role of the bedroom was aptly characterized by an eighteenth-century observer who wrote in 1799: "The lady's bedchamber is a sanctuary which no stranger is permitted to enter. It would be an act of the greatest possible indecorum to go into it, unless the visitor were upon a very familiar footing with the family."

The evolution of the bed closely parallels that of the bedroom: the more ceremonious the function of the bedroom, the grander and more opulent the bed. Because history repeats itself—especially with respect to decorative styles—a brief survey of the historical development of the bed offers a wealth of decorating ideas. Since time immemorial, the primary objective of the bed has been to cushion the sleeper from the hard ground or floor. For many centuries people achieved this objective merely by filling sacks with straw or hay. These rudimentary beds were the precursors of mattresses as we know them, and the tradition lives on: a mattress covered in simple homespun or ticking and placed directly on the floor has an inviting, back-to-basics appeal.

In ancient Egypt, Greece, and Rome beds were lightweight and portable so they could be moved about multipurpose rooms with ease. Egyptian beds had simple wooden frames covered with webbing and topped by a hard, raised headrest, the purpose of which was to preserve stiffly coiffed hairdos rather than to provide comfort like the soft pillows used today. The beds were often draped with mosquito netting or less expensive fishing nets to keep out insects. This simple practice is inexpensive to re-create, and it imparts a soft, romantic look whether the netting surrounds an elegant Egyptian Revival bed or a plain mattress. Greek beds resembled couches and were used both for sleeping and for reclining on while dining. Headboards and ornamental pillows not only made them more comfortable but were also indicators of status. Sinuously curved and often lavishly decorated, Roman beds were similar to their Greek counterparts. Revivals or reproductions of these beds can lend a neoclassical look to any bedroom.

The tradition of movable furniture continued into the medieval period and endured among the poorer classes well into the eighteenth century. During the early Middle Ages, landowners led a rather peripatetic existence: to oversee their holdings they regularly moved their entire households from property to property. Portability was therefore essential, and beds were for the most part simple affairs, consisting of a wooden base, low vertical posts, and a separate canopy that could be taken apart and folded into cases. The

8

status symbol in those days was less the bed than the bed hangings, which could be easily packed and transported. Fine textiles were rare and exorbitantly expensive, so wealthy landowners invested vast sums in these portable symbols of affluence. Thus began the love affair between the bed and its bedclothes, which has endured, in endless variations on the theme, to this day.

Renaissance beds ranged from those described by Montaigne in 1580 as "wretched little tables on which they throw planks . . . and you are very well lodged if you have a canopy," to grander ones, sometimes of elaborately carved wood, sometimes built into cupboardlike alcoves. Others featured posts and curtainlike hangings; these might be raised on a platform and flanked by chests that were used for storage as well as seating.

As time went on, beds became extremely large, not only to accommodate numerous occupants (it was common for several family members to sleep together) but also to create grand impressions, like the Great Bed of Ware, c. 1590, in which "four couples might cozily lie side by side, and thus without touching each other abide."

In the seventeenth century the predominant style was the rectangular, box-shaped bed, often referred to as a "French bedde." It featured a flying tester, or roof, either suspended from the ceiling or supported by posts, and covered with side hangings and a head cloth. In form it was influenced by state beds. Swathed in voluminous, extravagant hangings and raised on platforms, state beds were often encircled by a balustrade that permitted visitors to approach only so far. The height of the bed rose in proportion to its grandeur and theatricality. The late-seventeenth- and early-eighteenth-century published designs of Daniel Marot, court architect to William of Orange, popularized the style in both England and France.

At the other end of the social spectrum, the constraints of one-room living yielded expedient solutions and innovative designs. Sometimes ordinary chests filled with sacks of straw were used as impromptu beds. There also were beds that when folded up turned into other pieces of furniture, such as wooden chests. These innovations found their way into wealthy homes as well. An awestruck visitor to the Palazzo de' Medici in 1644 described a "conceited chayre . . . which turned into a bed, a bolster, a table, and a couch."

Until the Renaissance elaborate carving had been reserved for state beds. But by the eighteenth century, beds were as much the domain of the furniture maker as the curtain maker and the upholsterer. Although hangings did not diminish in importance, bed posts were now often intended for full view, and therefore began to be quite decorative. A profusion of designs for both bedsteads and hangings were published and circulated widely among a burgeoning middle class. The production of less expensive textiles enabled more people to feel like royalty when they went to bed.

The bed's lofty position in the hierarchy of interior furnishings is attested to by an architectural drawing of a London house (c. 1774) depicting a sumptuously draped bed—one of the few pieces of furniture deemed significant enough to merit inclusion (page 10). And, as British furniture maker George Hepplewhite wrote in The Cabinet-Maker and Upholsterer's Guide, 1788, beds "are an article of much importance, as well on account of the great expense attending them, as the variety of shapes, and the high degree of elegance which may be shewn in them."

By the middle of the eighteenth century state beds were still de rigueur in royal settings, but fashion was shifting away from them as a model. Soon there was no end of different designs to choose from: beds with or without posts, each with its own style of canopy and hangings. As historian Eileen Harris has written, "The imposing opulence of the past was cast off for coquettish confections."

Toward the end of the eighteenth century one of the more popular confections available was the lit à la polonaise, which featured a domed canopy. A particularly exotic one was fitted with mirrored parts that

9

reflected the view out the window, so that, when lying on it, one felt as though he or she "was actually lying out in the open air," as an observer wrote in 1786. In the 1793 edition of The Cabinet-Maker and Upholsterer's Drawing-Book, Thomas Sheraton published a design for a "summer bed" in "two compartments . . . intended for a nobleman or gentleman and his lady to sleep separately in hot weather," as well as his version of the famed lit à bateau, or boat-shaped bed. Various forms of daybeds and sofa beds appeared, used for seating, lounging, sleeping, or receiving visitors in a salon. There were folding field and campaign beds that were intended for military use and traveling but were also ideal for small rooms. Sheraton also designed beds that folded conveniently into a linen press or cupboard. Owing to its newly retrieved privacy, the bedroom was a perfect place to indulge in the eighteenth-century passion for folly and fantasy. Chippendale created beds in the Gothic and chinoiserie styles, and George Smith later designed romanticized twiglike bedsteads.

Hangings became equally whimsical during the eighteenth century. Then, as now, they created the feeling that one was entering a self-contained world when climbing into bed. One eighteenth-century observer expressed that feeling when he wrote that the bed was like "a room in itself, with four posts, flowered curtains for walls, a chintz tester for ceiling, and steps conducting one into an acre of billowy bolstered bliss!"

LONGITUDINAL SECTION OF A MANSION, C. 1774, BY JOHN YENN. AN ELABORATE CANOPY BED IS ONE OF THE FEW FURNISHINGS INCLUDED IN THIS ARCHITECTURAL RENDERING.

The impact of hangings was as important from inside the bed as from outside. Story-telling fabrics, such as French toiles de Jouy, which depicted allegorical, exotic, or pastoral tales, as well as topical events like the craze for hot-air ballooning, were all the rage as bed hangings in the eighteenth century. A love of the imaginary and exotic persisted into the nineteenth century, as exemplified by the Regency and Empire penchant for tented rooms and beds. When Mary Russell Mitford visited Rosedale Cottage, an English cottage orné, in the early nineteenth century, she observed that each room was differently and fancifully decorated. Some were "swarming with furniture crocodiles and sphinxes. . . . They sleep in Turkish tents and dine in a Gothic chapel."

Undoubtedly one of the most famous beds of the early nineteenth century was that of Madame Récamier (page 11) in Paris. Privileged visitors to the city felt their stay was incomplete if they did not see this latest example of the neoclassical style. Mary Berry was no exception. After her visit in 1802, she wrote: "Went to the house of Mme. Récamier. We were resolved not to leave Paris without seeing what is called the most elegant house in it, fitted up in the new style. . . . It is certainly fitted up with all the récherché and expense possible in what is now called le goût antique. . . . Her bed is reckoned the most beautiful in Paris—it too, is of mahogany, enriched with ormolu and bronze, and raised upon two steps of the same wood. Over the whole bed was thrown a great coverlid or veil of fine plain muslin with rows of narrow gold lace at each end, the muslin embroidered as a border. The curtains were muslin, trimmed with and worked like the coverlid suspended from a sort of carved couronne de roses and tucked up in drapery upon the wall, against which the bed stood."

During the Victorian period. with its penchant for eclecticism. post beds with elaborate hangings were produced in every revival style imaginable. At the same time, a heightened concern for hygiene. and the desire to stamp out bed bugs and other vermin, resulted in the wide-scale production of metal bedsteads—typically iron or brass. If the showy hangings of the past were symbolic of rank, these metal beds were tangible symbols of the latest social values. The Victorians paid great attention to the decoration of the bedroom. As a nineteenth-century prescriptive writer admonished, "The sleeping room, in which nearly half of one's life is passed, ought to be as pretty as a sitting room."

The same holds true today. We, too, perceive the bedroom as a sanctuary and often spend a good half of our time in it, gravitating toward it more than any other room in the house. And the way we decorate the bedroom is symbolic of who we really are.

Comfort is paramount in today's bedroom. Yet everyone's idea of comfort is different, ranging from spare minimalism to cluttered coziness. Whatever your definition of comfort, it will dictate the mood you wish to create. When decorating your bedroom it is important to identify a starting point, whether

THE BEDROOM OF MADAME RÉCAMIER, 1802, BY SIR ROBERT SMIRKE.

a piece of furniture, a wall treatment, or a specific fabric. One way to take you straight to the heart of the matter is to begin with the only truly essential piece of bedroom furniture—the bed. The style of bed you choose will affect the entire decorative scheme of the room. For example, a mattress and box spring placed on the floor immediately creates a pared-down, contemporary feeling that can then be dressed up as little or as much as you like. A traditional four-poster instantly imparts a period look that either can be carried out to the letter in all the details of the room, including the bed hangings, wall treatment, and other furniture, or can be set in contrast to the other elements in the room for an eclectic feeling.

There are a vast range of bedsteads to choose from and several ways to go about getting one: you can buy one, either antique or new; reclaim or adapt a "found object"; or make one. If you want a period or eclectic look, turn the search into a treasure hunt. First, to familiarize your eye with the wealth of possibilities, begin by looking at prints and paintings from different periods, vintage photographs, or antique pattern books, all of which vividly record interiors of the past in meticulous detail. Then embark on the search itself, which will spark your imagination even further. Among the styles of bedsteads you may come across are baroque, rococo, nineteenth-century campaign beds (pages 34, 43, 54, 109), Egyptian Revival (pages 16–17), Biedermeier (pages 18, 24), Empire (pages 25, 58), chinoiserie, Victorian turned metal (pages 26, 44, 67), Art Nouveau, Art Deco, Shaker (pages 28, 69), and all manner of French daybeds (pages 33, 45).

Whereas authentic period beds may require a substantial investment, nineteenth-century revivals of various styles, including Queen Anne, rococo, and neoclassical, or twentieth-century copies are much more affordable and have the same effect. Although you would not want to tamper with a mint-condition antique in any way, a rusted Victorian sleigh bed or a Regency field bed in less than pristine condition can be brought back to life with a touch of paint or gilding.

Scavenging through architectural salvage depots, flea markets, and auction houses may yield a wonderful "found object" that may not have originally been intended as a bed frame but that has great decorative potential. Reclaiming a found object can help stretch a tight budget and you will have enormous fun in the process. For example, you can convert a fragment of decoratively carved period paneling or a trumeau (a mirrored panel topped by a painting) into an imaginative headboard either by using it as is or by stripping it, painting it, or embellishing it with gold leaf, and then attaching it to the wall or directly to the bed. Similarly, an old corona or tester, now separated from the bed it originally partnered, can serve as a basic structure for hangings and add cachet to the simplest bed. Even a mantelpiece can be transformed into a headboard simply by filling in the opening with upholstery or an antique wallpaper screen.

If you prefer to create a more contemporary feeling, there are countless alternatives to choose from, such as sleek molded-wood headboards, bold wrought-iron frames painted in primary colors, naturalistic rattan or raffia bedsteads, rustic designs in stripped pine, painted or color-washed wood frames in striking asymmetrical shapes, and fluidly bent wire frames fashioned to look like molten silver or Gaudiesque fantasies.

Once you have chosen a bed, whether framed or unframed, you can either "dress it up" with a canopy, swags, festoons, draped hangings, and so on, or leave it "undressed," wearing only its basic bedclothes—sheets, pillow-

cases, and blanket or comforter. For extra flair, inexpensive plain sheets and pillowcases can be monogrammed with your initials, appliquéd with lace fragments, or dipped in tea to give them an Old World feeling.

The variety of sheets and pillowcases available today is virtually limitless, ranging from basic white, bordered or unbordered, which can be either ironed crisply (pages 18, 23, 26) or left seductively wrinkled (pages 108, 109, 112), to earthy beige homespun with scalloped or stand-up European borders, perhaps ornamented with wooden, plastic, or fabric-covered buttons, or casual or formal bows (pages 43, 57). As for prints, country or windowpane checks, demure or bold stripes, mattress ticking, small- or large-scale patterns of all kinds, Matisse-inspired designs splashed with vibrant color, basket weaves, and Indian or Oriental motifs are just a few of the options.

Simply by dressing the bed you will begin to give the room its decorative flavor. For instance, an early American crewelwork coverlet will simulate the feeling of the "best chamber" in a Queen Anne house: rural-style prints or dimity will suggest a hamlet by the sea; regimental stripes paired with sheer gauze or muslin will conjure up the ambience of the nineteenth-century Swedish countryside (page 68); and a sea of glazed chintz will steep the room in Victorian charm. Draping a boldly striped sheet over the bed will create a neoclassical look. For an updated, less formal variation on the theme, use sheets with broad bands of color. Combining small- and large-scale striped floral patterns (page 50) will lend the room a touch of old-fashioned femininity.

If you have a period canopy bed—or have created the look of one—and you wish to dress it in a period style, the many eighteenth- and nineteenth-century furniture makers' and curtain makers' pattern books are excellent sources and can be used as a starting point for your own interpretation. You can either copy a design exactly, borrow a single element, or combine details from various designs. For example, you can re-create a neoclassical look by topping the canopy with a gilded crown and hanging silk flecked with Napoleonic bees from it. Or you might select just one typical detail of Empire style, such as bow and arrow finials, rosettes, or heavy rope tassels, to give plain hangings a regal touch. By using your imagination, you can adapt the ideas in these designs in other ways besides hangings. For example, a gathered swag, like the ones commonly used on nineteenth-century testers, can be attached to the sides of a simple box-spring frame to soften its severe shape.

Although it is rare to find an entire set of period hangings intact, you may come across all sorts of fragments at flea markets, auctions, or antiques shops, such as crewelwork panels, antique tapestry, vintage cottons, embroidered velvet, and antique toile de Jouy (page 51), all of which add great character to any bed. You might prefer simply to top the bed with a vintage coverlet (pages 23, 49), an American or English patchwork quilt (page 43), a turn-of-the-century flowered chintz faded from years of laundering, or second-hand linens full of old-fashioned charm (pages 18, 36).

The wall treatment you choose can give even the most nondescript bedroom a distinct style. By covering the walls with paneling, whether period or fashioned out of inexpensive medium-density fiberboard (MDF), and either leaving it plain, ornamenting it with ribbons and garlands, or painting panoramic scenes on it, you can achieve looks that suggest a Georgian town house, a Victorian library (page 110), a Tuscan villa (page 67), or a French folly (pages 128–129).

Another way to effect the mood you want is by painting the walls. A mural of a classical garden simulates the atmosphere of a formal European courtyard; a seascape creates the illusion of sleeping at the water's edge. Marbleizing the walls captures the opulence of an Italian palazzo or a tsar's summer palace. A trompe l'oeil cornice of graceful swags and garlands adds architectural interest and charm.

Similar effects can be achieved with wallpaper or fabric. For a bedroom with an exotic view, try a scenic, or panoramic, wallpaper. For a country garden ambience, consider a delicate floral- or leaf-patterned wallpaper or fabric. For a soft, romantic look, drape the walls with new or antique lace in gentle folds. Walls painted in a solid color or papered in a subtle stripe serve as a neutral background for favorite paintings, prints, or photographs (pages 56, 57, and 71).

Any number of floor treatments are appropriate for the bedroom. Leave wooden floorboards bare for a period look; paint them or stencil them for a country feeling. Mix and match needlework scatter rugs for color and accent. Carpeting, either plain or patterned, warms the floor, making it pleasant for walking on in bare feet. Natural-fiber matting, with or without a contrasting border, creates a rustic look; dhurries or kilims add an ethnic touch. If you are lucky enough to find a well-worn Aubusson or Savonnerie carpet, let its faded floral patterns dictate the color scheme of the entire room. Fragments of such carpets are often less expensive and can be used as accent rugs.

Window treatments are equally varied. Shutters have the advantage of affording maximum light when open and complete privacy when closed. Period or reproduction shutters are available in a wide range of styles, from raised and fielded Georgian paneling to delicately carved versions to the simple louvered contemporary kind. You can leave old shutters as you find them, or strip them, distress them, or rub them with paint. Painting a perspective scene on shutters or plain shades creates the feeling of a room with a view even when the shutters are closed or the shades are drawn. Curtain fabric can either match or contrast that of the bed. If you have a canopy bed, you can unify the room by repeating the design of the tester and hangings at the windows. Or you can loosely drape the fabric from a rod and tie it back to one side asymmetrically, dressed up with a tassel (pages 18, 36), decorative finial (page 23), or rosette (page 27). Ruffled festoon shades lend softness and femininity to a room.

13

The vanity, or dressing table, is at once a practical and decorative addition to any bedroom. You can either find a vintage one and top it with a splendid mirror, or make your own from plywood or MDF and cover it with fabric in as simple or elaborate a way as you like (pages 78, 83, 86, 89). The idea of displaying collections of trinkets and baubles on a vanity is not new. Describing Queen Charlotte's dressing table in 1767, the eighteenth-century diarist Mrs. Lybbe Powys noted that "on her toilet [there were] beside the gold plate innumerable 'knick-knacks'." When you are not wearing your favorite costume jewelry, adorn the vanity with it. Hanging ropes of beads or faux pearls from a mirror and clipping earrings to a lampshade (pages 74, 80, 81, 89) not only looks pretty but also keeps your baubles within easy reach. Antique cosmetic jars, tinted glass bottles with gleaming silver, brass, or vermeil tops, differently shaped fragrance flasks, and oversize perfumers' jars with shiny brass spigots are both beautiful and useful accessories for the vanity. The bottles and jars that house the potions and lotions you use on a daily basis, such as Chanel's bold geometric black-and-white plastic or Clinique's translucent green ones, can also be extremely decorative. No vanity is complete without a mirror, whether the hand-held Victorian variety (page 78) or a dainty lacquered neoclassical mirror with miniature drawers. You might consider dressing up an ordinary mirror by reviving the eighteenth-century practice of draping it in fabric gathered with bows.

14

LUXE ET INDIGENCE, C. 1810, BY LOUIS-MARIE LANTÉ.
A PAISLEY SHAWL, HAT BOXES, AND A FOLDING CAMPAIGN BED
TRANSFORM THIS GARRET INTO A BEDROOM WITH STYLE.

Perhaps the greatest challenge in decorating the bedroom is devising enough easily accessible storage space to accommodate clothes, shoes, linens, luggage, books, writing materials, and so forth. There are two different but equally viable approaches: concealing and revealing. You can either store everything neatly out of view in closets, cabinets, bureaus, chests, and so on, or you can exploit the inherently ornamental qualities of some of the things you are storing and integrate them into the room's decor.

There are all sorts of ways to hide things decoratively. Cabinet or closet doors can be constructed from fragments of real paneling, or you can create the same look using a synthetic material. For a fraction of the cost, you can give ordinary doors lots of character by adding picture-frame molding, painting them with a plain or faux finish, or turning to historical techniques, such as découpage. You might let the need to mask uninteresting doors be the impetus to create a sort of updated print room by gluing period bed, bed hanging, or fashion designs on the doors and linking the designs with wallpaper borders. Or you might consider ornamenting doors with masses of framed prints or sepia photographs. Mirrored closet doors help increase the sense of space in small rooms.

The alternative is to give pride of place to favorite possessions. Designer Lillian Williams has infused a New York apartment with the romance of an eighteenth-century French bedchamber. Among an array of captivating period furnishings she casually displays a cherished collection of antique shoes and hat boxes (pages 128–29). Antique clothing, from eighteenth-century waistcoats to 1920s beaded shifts picked up at flea markets, make a strong decorative statement when hung on closet doors or from open racks. Even the most common objects have great decorative effect when massed together, such as the handkerchiefs tied with ribbons on page 96. Towels or trousers can be draped over mahogany, faux-bamboo, or painted wooden racks. Even the rungs of a wooden ladder can provide storage with style (page 98).

Again, found objects come in handy, this time in the guise of imaginative storage containers. Vintage traveling trunks (page 98), often fitted with shirt or shoe drawers and even with ironing boards; antique bandboxes covered in period wallpaper; leather travel cases fitted with compartments for vanity bottles (page 93); antique Chinese wedding trunks; country baskets; rattan chests (page 112); and inexpensive laundry baskets (page 96), whether used as is or dressed up with tassels and antique ribbons, are just a few of the many objects that can solve storage problems while adding decorative interest to the room. Ordinary shoe boxes covered in fabric or wallpaper and hand labeled for easy reference make attractive, inexpensive storage containers. Either pile them up from floor to ceiling or build simple shelving for them.

Freestanding storage units offer great flexibility, decorative impact, and, hopefully, investment potential. An antique carved French or country armoire (page 98) or an English linen press is of course ideal for storing garments. But you can also buy an inexpensive unfinished armoire and paint it or cover it with fabric panels. A striped cotton tent will evoke the atmos-phere of a seaside resort at the turn of the century, while serving as an easily portable closet.

Today, as throughout much of history, many people live in one-room spaces, from large lofts to intimate studio apartments. Incorporating the bed into such all-in-one spaces requires a bit of decorative ingenuity. You can either showcase the bed (pages 109, 111) or conceal it. Contemporary trundle beds (page 112) and sofa beds double as daytime seating for entertaining guests, reading, working, or just relaxing. The rooms shown on pages 106–21 offer a host of ideas for working within spatial constraints to create the environment that best suits your taste and life style both night and day.

As the most private room of the house, the bedroom is one place where your imagination need know no bounds. If you have always wanted to sleep under the stars, why not cover the ceiling with a shimmering miniature galaxy? If you long for the romance of 1,001 Arabian nights, nothing is stopping you from tenting the room with a gauzy fabric ornamented with tassels. If you fantasize about spending your nights in an English castle, find an antique four-poster fit for a king. If you dream of dozing in a breezy tent on the beach or of being gently lulled to sleep in a punt floating down a river in the English countryside, create the setting illusionistically with paint. If you find the mysterious sights of a North African spice market irresistibly seductive, use its brilliant color palette to evoke the atmosphere. Whether you crave the sultry exoticism of a bedroom perched on the edge of a Bangkok canal (page 130), the sensuality of a Belle Epoque boudoir, or the homey comfort of a hammock in the backyard (page 135), the pages that follow will show you countless ways to translate your flights of fancy into reality.

BARE ESSENTIALS
THE BED

When decorating the bedroom, the range of possibilities can be daunting. But if you begin with the only truly essential piece of furniture, the bed, the mood you wish to create will follow naturally from there.

• THE MATTRESS: For a stripped-down, back-to-basics look, simply place a mattress on the floor (page 27).

• THE FRAME: Searching for a decorative bedstead is a scavenger's dream. For a period or eclectic look, let the pages of history be your guide. Four-poster beds range in style from elaborately carved Gothic (page 22) to painted neoclassical (page 41), majestic Empire (pages 25, 58), and Georgian mahogany (page 51). Or choose sleigh beds—from provincial Biedermeier (page 18) to a nineteenth-century painted version with swan supports and lyre-shaped feet (page 16) to ormolu-encrusted Empire (page 25). Period campaign beds like the tented Regency one on page 34 bring the spirit of the outdoors into any bedroom. Charming Victorian metal bedsteads, either adorned with graceful metal swirls (pages 26, 44) or plain (page 77), are easy to find.

• THE FOUND OBJECT: All sorts of objects can be reclaimed and used as bed frames. Flea markets, antiques shops, auction houses, and architectural salvage depots make excellent hunting grounds. Old French paneling, a mirror, a period trumeau, or an ornamental painting can be mounted on the wall as a headboard. A carved mantelpiece, an oversize period picture frame, or a pair of flat pilasters can be transformed into a headboard by upholstering the middle with fabric. Attaching a corona to the wall over the bed (page 44) eliminates the need for a frame. Even Venetian barge poles can be converted into decorative posts to create the look of the bed on page 53. Ordinary materials, such as garden trellises, metal, and wire, make imaginative, low-cost frames and/or headboards. Curtain rods, topped with finials and then painted or gilded, can be used as bed posts to achieve looks similar to those on pages 41, 42, and 51.

• THE HEADBOARD: Comfort is essential in a bedroom, and for many, an upholstered headboard is an obvious way to achieve it. To make your own, cut the shape you prefer out of plywood and cover it with your favorite fabric or an antique textile fragment, such as a piece of old linen, embroidered velvet, crewelwork, toile de Jouy, or tapestry. For a heraldic look, embroider an oversize monogram on heavy cotton. Contemporary headboards are available in a wide range of materials, including rattan, metal, and wood. Use slabs of wood to create a rustic frame (pages 32, 35).

With its lyre-shaped feet and swan-shaped frame, this Empire-period, Egyptian Revival bed discovered by Genevieve Weaver was doubtless the inspiration for the fanciful neoclassical decor of this room.

The Biedermeier bed in London picture dealer Stephanie Hoppen's New York apartment provides a majestic setting for her extensive collection of antique linens. Oversize, old-fashioned pillowcases and a topsheet framed with a delicate border ending in tiny points add period style. (LEFT)

18

A nineteenth-century daybed with faux-bamboo posts and molding is the focal point of this bedroom in Anna Fendi's Roman palazzo. The soft stripe covering the walls, ceiling, and door imparts a tentlike feeling to the room.

19

With its trompe l'oeil floor tiles, this bedroom at
Fighine Castle in the Italian countryside requires
little decoration besides a scrolling wrought-iron
bedstead with brass ornaments and finials.
(FACING PAGE)

Some types of beds don't even need mattresses to
provide a good night's sleep, such as this decoratively
painted and ornamented one on the island of Lamu
near the coast of Kenya. (RIGHT)

21

With its rhythmic trefoil arches and lacy carving, designer Tessa Kennedy's dramatic Gothic Revival bed is like a room within a room. Frothy white dust ruffles, coverlet, and pillowcases lighten its architectural mass. (LEFT)

The warm colors of a late-nineteenth-century painted bedstead are picked up in an antique Welsh floral-patterned quilt and in the vintage French silk curtain that tops the delicate cotton fabric draping the window in this bedroom designed by Mimmi O'Connell of Port of Call. (FACING PAGE)

22

With its delicate neoclassical wall decoration and boldly shaped Biedermeier furniture, this bedroom at Hylinge, in Sweden, is an example of how people decorated in the past, incorporating furniture of a slightly later date to keep in step with the latest fashion.

Shaped like a boat and made of mahogany with gilt-bronze mounts, this sumptuous Empire bed in the château of the Duc de Caraman is similar to the famed lit à bateau of Madame Récamier.
(ABOVE AND RIGHT)

26

Designer Mimmi O'Connell has
given a contemporary look to this
Victorian metal bedstead by leaving
its frame exposed rather than
draping it with hangings as it might
have been in the past. The stark
lines of the frame are offset by
the ornamental headboard and
footboard, the antique cotton
coverlet, the floral-patterned carpet,
and the delicately embroidered
crewelwork fabric covering walls
and ceiling.

With its clean, graphically interesting lines, Shaker furniture offers a host of ideas for simple yet imaginative bedroom design. For instance, the tradition of hanging furniture and clothes from a strip of molding nailed to the wall is both a space-saving and a decorative device. (FACING PAGE)

The choice of bed is sometimes dictated by the atmosphere of a room. In this centuries-old bedroom, with its rough-hewn ceiling beams, whitewashed walls, and weathered stone floor, what could be more appropriate than a time-worn wrought-iron bedstead? (RIGHT)

29

This bedroom, designed by architect Charles Jencks, evokes the spirit of the work of Scottish architect Charles Rennie Mackintosh (see page 31). The headboard, perforated with a series of tiny squares, sets the decorative theme of the room. The motif is repeated in the door frames and shelving.

30

The bedroom at Hill House in Helensburgh, Scotland, designed in 1904 by architect Charles Rennie Mackintosh, is a study in the use of basic geometric forms for decorative effect. Little squares balance elongated rectangles, and the rectangular forms are in exquisite proportion to the semicircular arch of the alcove.

Constructed out of sturdy slabs of distressed, bleached wood, with the posts innovatively cut on an angle, this bed's natural look is echoed in the rustic leather chair and the bare floorboards.

32

Designer Carolyn Quartermaine
has transformed an eclectic
assemblage of found objects,
including a pair of French chairs
and a daybed, into unique treasures.
By leaving the original gilding intact
and upholstering the pieces in her
own hand-painted fabrics, she has
created a play between the historical
and the contemporary. A vintage
electrical heater demonstrates the
decorative charm of reclaimed
everyday objects.

33

34

Campaign beds, like this
sumptuously tented Regency one,
are ideal for small spaces and
have the added advantage of being
collapsible, so that they can be
moved around or stored away
when necessary.

Soft earth tones and natural materials can create a warm, rustic look in any setting, from the countryside to the city.

WRAPPED IN COMFORT

DRESSING THE BED

Having chosen the bed, the next step is to dress it, starting with the underclothes (sheets and pillowcases) and proceeding to the outer garments (blanket, quilt, coverlet, bedspread, hangings, and an array of trimmings). This chapter presents an entire wardrobe of bedclothes, from romantic mosquito netting to cheerful floral-patterned cotton to sensuous silk.

• LINENS: The most basic, and affordable, approach to dressing the bed is to leave it in its underclothes. Ordinary white sheets, either crisply starched or seductively rumpled, when allowed to cascade onto the floor in soft folds, can transform a bare mattress into an oasis of comfort. In contrast, tightly wrapped sheets have a neat, tailored look (page 27). There are printed sheets to suit every taste. For a neoclassical look, try a simple stripe; chintzlike floral prints lend a Victorian feel (page 44); animal prints have an exotic allure (page 47); plaids, checks, and other bright, multicolored patterns suggest the fresh country air. The advantage of dressing your bed with sheets is that you can wholly change the look with the seasons or with your mood without great expense.

• COVERS: A coverlet or blanket can complement the patterns of your sheets and pillowcases or contrast with them for a more eclectic look (page 49). Throws, from faux fur to Victorian needlework (page 109), lend an elegant warmth.

• HANGINGS: Hangings can cloak even the most ordinary bed in romance, drama, or regality. Simply by suspending mosquito netting or sheer starched voile from the ceiling and draping it around the bed, you can suggest the ambience of the colonial Caribbean, the British Raj in India, or an African safari camp (pages 47, 132). Whatever the style of hangings you wish to create, from whimsical eighteenth-century French swags (pages 38, 128) to neoclassical tenting (page 54), period pattern books are an excellent source of design ideas.

You don't have to invest in an antique canopy bed to create the look of period hangings. You can achieve the same effect by attaching a fabric roof or period corona to the ceiling and hanging curtains or sheets from it (page 45); by constructing a frame out of wooden or synthetic cornicing; by draping hangings from a decorative wall rosette (pages 40, 44, 48); or by making a Renaissance-inspired, freestanding canopy (page 40).

• FINISHING TOUCHES: New or antique decorative tassels (pages 38, 45, 50, 51), ribbons, fabric bows (pages 43, 52) or rosettes (page 78), fringes (page 45), and contrasting fabric borders are just a few of the trimmings that add finishing touches to bed hangings.

38

PAGES 36 AND 37

By rotating sheets and pillowcases from her cherished collection of period bedclothes. Stephanie Hoppen can continually change the look of her bed while complementing her London bedroom's antique style, which is created by the collection of pictures, including images of putti from the seventeenth, eighteenth, and nineteenth centuries.

Updating an eighteenth-century French tradition, fashion designer Karl Lagerfeld has jauntily draped toile de Jouy hangings over the metal frame of the antique bed in his Roman home. Ropy tassels add a touch of whimsy. The use of complementary fabrics for the headboard and bedspread is visually refreshing. (LEFT AND ABOVE)

In fashion designer Bill Blass's Connecticut bedroom, chocolate-brown walls with white trim make the perfect backdrop for a vintage brown-and-white American quilt, which tops a whimsically shaped brown-and-white striped bed. A spiral library staircase leading nowhere, here functioning as a piece of sculpture, brings the play on brown and white to a witty climax.

39

A Renaissance idea meets a contemporary interpretation in this canopy suspended directly from the ceiling over a basic platform bed in architect Andrea Cenci's bedroom. The side hangings ingeniously double as window drapery. (BELOW)

40

A simple, inexpensive way to achieve the soft, romantic look of bed hangings is to drape gauzy white cotton from a rosette on the wall. Ruffled window curtains and a tablecloth that puddles gently on the floor also contribute to the airy softness of Francesco Miani d'Angoris's bedroom. (ABOVE)

*For London antiques dealer
Christopher Gibbs, falling asleep in
this neoclassical bed must be an
ethereal experience. Its delicately
painted porcelain posts support a
carved and gilded tester. The
luxurious satin hangings are
covered with painted rosebuds.
A nineteenth-century embroidered
Indian coverlet adds an exotic
Eastern touch.*

41

When designing the hangings for the canopy bed in fashion designer Valentino's London bedroom, Roger Banks-Pye of Colefax and Fowler kept them simple, so as not to detract from the massive bed's elegantly carved frame. Suspended from rings, the unlined cream linen side hangings and head cloth can be easily opened and closed. The same linen is used for the sun-ray-pleated tester and its central rosette.

42

The rustic charm of this bedroom in the Italian countryside home of Francesco Miani d'Angoris is enhanced by the comfy, overstuffed pillowcases tied nonchalantly with decorative bows, like soft potato sacks. (ABOVE)

Contrasting patterns create a visual feast in this bedroom designed by David Mlinaric. The nineteenth-century metal campaign bed is dressed in a star-studded antique patchwork quilt and striped hangings, while the walls are covered in a floral-patterned paper that adds a touch of botanical freshness to the room. (RIGHT)

43

The gilded coronas mounted on the wall above a pair of nineteenth-century English wrought-iron and brass beds impart a regal touch to this bedroom in rural Italy designed by Mimmi O'Connell. The box springs, covered in a different striped fabric than that of the hangings and dust ruffles, have been made into a decorative feature. (BELOW)

44

The old-fashioned charm of a Victorian wrought-iron daybed served as the inspiration for the decor of this enchanting bedroom. Working with a blue-and-white color scheme, Port of Call imaginatively combined plaids, stripes, and floral patterns that have the look of Chinese porcelain to achieve such inviting results. (ABOVE)

In this California bedroom a fabric-covered, lambrequin-shaped corona suspended from the ceiling has transformed an antique daybed into a luxurious sleeping alcove. The golden hangings, lined with exuberant chintz and trimmed with plush tassels, beckon one inside, as do an inviting mound of pillows and an intriguing portrait in an oval frame.

45

Airily clad in cream-and-blue cotton hangings, the tall canopy bed in this Barbados bedroom · designed by Nicholas Haslam promises cool repose on the hottest Caribbean nights.

46

Even if you don't live in the tropics, you can create the exotic atmosphere of this bedroom on the island of Lamu by covering the bed in zebra-patterned sheets, suspending mosquito netting from the ceiling, and hanging bamboo shades on the windows.

Suspending a single length of fabric from a pole nailed to the wall above the bed and draping it gently over two gold rosettes imparts neoclassical elegance to any bedroom, whether the bed is of the period or not.

48

In this highly original bedroom designed by Port of Call, striped cotton is casually wound around the frame of the intricately carved nineteenth-century Indonesian four-poster bed. The boldly colored and printed sheets, pillowcases, and antique quilts create a potpourri of patterns.

49

A Regency-style canopy creates a cozy nook for this simply dressed bed. The designer of the room, Sally Metcalfe of George Spencer, has linked the two by covering the headboard with the same fabric as the canopy. A muted, striped floral wall covering serves as a soft background for the large Victorian needlework portraits of animals. All of these elements join forces to give warmth, character, and great charm to the room.

50

Eighteenth-century toile de Jouy hangings and matching bedspread adorn the author's English neoclassical mahogany bed. Printed with story-telling scenes, the fabric provides great visual interest, whether one is lying on the bed or seated in one of the painted antique chairs, which are upholstered in fragments of a different toile de Jouy pattern.

51

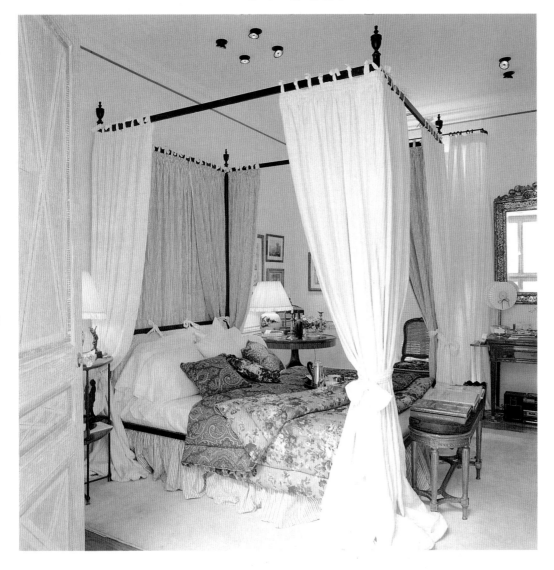

Designer Monika Apponyi has dressed this simple metal bed frame with casual elegance in hangings that tie on. White cotton on the outside but striped on the inside for contrast, the hangings cascade voluptuously onto the floor. The striped fabric is also used for the bed ruffle and the bolster, which ties on to the frame just like the hangings.

Mimmi O'Connell has whimsically transported the spirit of Venice to this London bedroom via the eighteenth-century Italian bed, the posts of which resemble the barge poles of that dreamy city. The crown and hangings of blue-and-white striped cotton are echoed in the Fortuny-inspired pattern stenciled on the walls.

53

DREAMSCAPES
WALL REVERIES

Whether you want the walls of your bedroom to serve as a subtle background for a collection of paintings or to draw attention to themselves, the only limit to decorating them is your own imagination. From wallpaper to paneling to elaborate trompe l'oeil scenes, this chapter offers a host of ways to turn your walls into a dreamscape.

♦ *PAINT: Walls painted a solid color function as a backdrop, setting off and complementing a bedroom's decorative scheme. But you can also treat your bedroom walls as a blank canvas on which to paint the illusion of a lush garden, a seascape, or any other setting, however fanciful (page 67), in which you've always longed to drift off to sleep. You can even paint a period headboard or canopy complete with hangings on the wall to simulate an expensive antique at a fraction of the cost. With paint you can also give your walls the cool richness of marble or the sun-baked feeling of stone. Use stencil patterns to achieve looks ranging from Swedish (page 68) to early-nineteenth-century American (page 90).*

♦ *ARCHITECTURAL ACCENTS: You can enhance the architectural interest of your bedroom walls by installing paneling (pages 38, 76, 100, 117), wainscoting (page 72), door frames, pilasters, arches, cornices, and so on. The* same effects can be approximated with picture-frame molding or simulated with paint (pages 56, 57, 68, 121). Architectural ornaments, such as garlands, bows, swags, and classical trophies, lend dignity to the plainest of walls.

♦ *WALLPAPER AND FABRIC: You can create almost any look by covering walls with paper or fabric. Delicate sprig prints, floral patterns (page 64), wide neoclassical-style stripes (pages 54, 59, 71), toiles de Jouy (page 60), checks (page 60), and panoramic scenes are just a few of the options.*

♦ *THE GALLERY EFFECT: If you have amassed a collection of paintings, drawings, posters, photographs, or ceramic plates, your bedroom walls may be the perfect place to showcase them.*

♦ *FLOOR AND WINDOW TREATMENTS: Virtually any floor treatment is appropriate for the bedroom, from cozy carpets, either solid-colored or patterned, to natural matting for an earthy feeling, to wooden floorboards, whether plain, painted, or stenciled. Needlework rugs, kilims, or painted floor cloths can be scattered over wooden floors for accent. Similarly, there are any number of window coverings to choose from, including painted or carved shutters, curtains, simple shades (page 70), and festive festoons and swags echoing the bed hangings (page 58).*

PAGES 54 AND 55

This neoclassical bedroom in Charlottenhof Castle, Potsdam, is as appealing today as the day it was created. Its simple yet elegant look can be re-created by forming a tent out of striped sheets or fabric and covering the walls and bed in the same material. Borders of passementerie, fabric, or wallpaper can be applied at cornice or baseboard level.

In this London bedroom designed by Anouska Hempel, the rich, deep red walls provide a dramatic backdrop for a fine collection of pictures evoking the spirit of Pompeii. The painted black borders suggest paneling. (RIGHT)

56

Hats and favorite photographs jauntily decorate the deep blue walls of the bedroom in Juliette Mole's London houseboat, anchored in the Thames. (BELOW)

A collection of Victorian engravings is the decorative focal point of this bedroom designed by Mimmi O'Connell. The ribbons from which they hang are made of the same material as the pillowcases, creating an interplay between bed and wall. (ABOVE)

58

Combining contemporary touches with authentic Empire furnishings and design elements, designers Osborne and Little have created their own hybrid style for this bedroom. For example, the window pelmet and the bed hangings are based on historical designs, but pairing a traditional Empire stripe and a boldly patterned contemporary chintz gives them a whole new look. The cross-banding on the tortoiseshell-papered walls was inspired by a Napoleonic military motif.

For this bedroom, designer Rupert Cavendish has re-created the Empire style with great fidelity. The clean, straight lines of the period furniture are appropriately set off by a handsomely striped wallpaper. Its trompe l'oeil cornice of tassels and rosettes repeats two of the major ornamental motifs in the room.

59

60

A checkered linen lends a cheerful country charm to a guest bedroom designed by Roger Banks-Pye of Colefax and Fowler for Valentino's London house. (BELOW)

For this guest bedroom in Valentino's London house Roger Banks-Pye boldly set the Russian-inspired neoclassical furniture designed by Chester Jones against an exuberant chinoiserie toile de Jouy wall covering, motifs of which are painted on the black doors. (ABOVE)

The patina of the centuries-old stone walls that lead to this bedroom in Earlshall Castle, Scotland, can be re-created by painting ordinary walls with a stone-block finish. Panels covered with antique crewelwork are not only decorative but protect the sleeper from cold drafts.

61

The leaf pattern stenciled on the walls of this
bedroom in Sam and Jeannie Chesterton's home
in Spain creates the impression that the bed is
nestled in an arboretum.

Sometimes the architecture of a space is so strong a decorative feature that it requires little in the way of additional adornment. In Federico Forquet's beautifully proportioned bedroom in the Tuscan hills, the only wall decoration necessary is the molding that subtly emphasizes the border between wall and ceiling.

63

The combination of a bold floral-patterned fabric and a contrasting stripe helps to make this cavernous and oddly shaped attic bedroom in the French countryside enticing and cozy. The floral wall covering predominates in the sleeping area of the room, while the stripe defines the sitting area.
(FACING PAGE AND RIGHT)

65

The beauty secret of th[...] [...]ntury
Swedish bedroom lies in the [...]
blue borders and delic[...]
the walls appear to be pan[...]
gives architectural distinction to the [...]
ordinary spaces. (FACING PAGE)

Even the severity of a Shaker bedroom can be
softened by hanging fabric on the wall and letting
it drape loosely. (RIGHT)

69

Designer Dot Spikings of Barefoot Elegance has created a light, airy feeling in this California bedroom by stippling the walls and ceiling a soft, neutral gray that serves as a cool background for the room's pastel palette. Cotton shades can be raised or lowered simply by tightening or loosening the patterned fabric bows.

70

This grand bedroom at Ardgowan, in Scotland, demonstrates how decorative it can be to display favorite objects and/or artworks on the walls. The charm lies both in the beauty of the individual objects and in the overall composition.

VANITY, VANITY
FROM BOTTLES TO BAUBLES

◆ *THE VANITY: Having a special place to indulge in the art of appearances—dressing up and making up—is a luxury, and that is what makes the vanity, or dressing table, so desirable. Vanities are also extremely decorative additions to the bedroom. They range in style from rococo (page 81) to Regency (page 75) to faux-bamboo Victorian (page 74) to Edwardian (page 80), and from simple country designs (page 86) to neoclassicism at its most refined. You can easily make your own vanity by covering any sort of table with fabric. Depending on the type of fabric you choose and the way you drape it, the effect can be tailored (page 86), frothy and romantic (page 83), or lacy (page 89). Writing desks double nicely as vanities, including eighteenth-century kneehole desks, rolltops, and drop leafs (page 87).*

◆ *MIRRORS: As Nina Campbell and Caroline Seebohm have written, the great American interior designer Elsie de Wolfe's New York home was affectionately termed the "little house of many mirrors" because, as she herself described it, "so much of its charm is the effect of skillfully managed reflections." Mirrors are an essential companion to any vanity. Their decorative role can be just as important as their functional one, and there are countless shapes, sizes, and framing materials to choose from, including simple arched*

country versions in plain wooden frames (this page), ovals or rectangles delicately framed in beribboned silver gilt (page 75) or painted wood (page 81), and the tripartite variety (pages 80, 84). Depending on how you place them, you can "manage" the reflection of favorite decorative details in the room.

◆ *COLLECTIONS: All sorts of items tend to accumulate in the bedroom, from grooming implements to cosmetics jars to family photos to books to jewelry. When grouped and displayed on vanities, bureaus, or night tables, these objects can contribute their own decorative touch to the room. A gleaming silver-backed Victorian grooming set (page 78), a collection of silver- or enamel-lidded cosmetics jars, or a group of antique perfume bottles (page 104) deserves pride of place on your vanity. But remember, the useful can be beautiful too, as the array of chunky plastic Chanel bottles, jars, and compacts on page 81 demonstrates. When not wearing your jewelry or hats, dress up your room with them by hanging ropes of pearls, necklaces, and hats from mirrors and clipping earrings to lampshades (pages 74, 80, 81, 82). Even an assortment of handbags makes a decorative statement when artfully displayed (page 80).*

73

PAGES 72 AND 73
Whitewashed walls, floors, ceiling, and furniture; overstuffed chairs, chaise longue, and pillows; and a profusion of mirrors all combine to give this bedroom in a Shelter Island cottage an airy, casual comfort. A painted chest, topped by a collection of lusterware jars and a pair of mirrors, doubles nicely as a vanity.

In designer Felicity Osborne's bedroom an elaborately painted Victorian dressing table with a tilting mirror and lots of drawers, nooks, and crannies is a decorative delight in and of itself. But its decorative impact has been further enhanced by the jewelry, bottles, jars, photographs, and silver-backed grooming set that adorn it. (LEFT)

A revival of the historical print-room technique transforms this minute alcove into a charming spot for a vanity. Miniature portraits ornament walls and cupboard doors. Similarly decorated hat boxes perched on a faux-bamboo Regency washstand provide attractive storage for all sorts of everyday necessities. (BELOW)

75

In print dealer Julia Boston's London bedroom an antique mirror framed with elaborately curling silver-gilt ribbons is the centerpiece of a three-dimensional still life consisting of paintings, mirrors, photographs, and assorted trinkets. The key to its decorative impact lies both in the selection of the objects, all of which express the owner's personal taste, and in their arrangement. (ABOVE)

A mahogany rolltop desk ornamented with bronze mounts turns this corner of a bedroom in Karl Lagerfeld's Roman home into a study. The painted and gilded period paneling behind the desk incorporates a built-in armoire. (LEFT)

Entering this bedroom in Ireland is like stepping back into the nineteenth century, thanks to the transfer-printed ceramics, windup alarm clock, and Victorian oil lamp atop the sturdy chest with its tilting round mirror. (FACING PAGE)

A vintage embroidered shawl turns a round table into a charming bedroom occasional table, on which Vicky Rothco has beautifully arranged a collection of antique blue-and-white porcelain pieces and a Victorian silver-backed grooming set. (BELOW)

Any ordinary table can be transformed into a decorative bedside table simply by covering it with fabric to the floor. For additional flair, the fabric can then be trimmed with bows, tassels, or fabric rosettes, such as the one over which the bed hangings are draped in this bedroom designed by Osborne and Little. (ABOVE)

Designer Andrea de Montal has used pretty floral-patterned fabrics to inspire a romantic aspect to this rustic setting. Period coverlets drape a round side table and a rectangular table on which family photographs are displayed. The inspiration for the decor may well have been the antique chintz covering the delightfully shaped Victorian sofa.

When not being used, the jewelry, hats, and handbags covering this painted Edwardian vanity moonlight as ornamental objects. The handbags are as useful as they are decorative. The one with the sunburst-framed clock eliminates the need for a bedside clock. Those shaped like chests of drawers double as jewelry boxes. All of the bags were designed by Anya Hindmarch.

80

A dainty nineteenth-century painted vanity table is almost obscured by a decorative clutter of lotions, potions, and baubles. Evening bags, shiny Chanel shopping bags, and a Valentino faux-leopard shoe pouch have all found new uses as storage containers for everything from pearls to headbands to eye pencils.

81

In this delightful room designed by Nina Campbell for Kate Vestey, a mahogany desk has been pressed into service as a commodious vanity. Cosmetics are efficiently, and decoratively, stored in fabric-lined baskets. A standing lamp provides a convenient perch for favorite straw hats.

84

This colorfully painted vanity table in the American Museum in Britain may inspire you to rummage through the attic or the local flea market for an old vanity and reclaim it by painting or stenciling it with the design of your choice.

85

Designer John Stefanidis has fitted out this
rectangular vanity and circular stool in matching
tailored suits. A sheet of glass protects the fabric
covering the top of the vanity. (RIGHT)

It is not surprising that floral designer Kenneth
Turner chose to decorate the bedside table in his
London bedroom with flowers, both fresh and
dried. Flowers often provide the finishing
touch to any decor. (BELOW)

86

Designer Joanna Wood has maximized the decorative potential of this handsome writing desk by using its drop leaf to display a collection of period porcelain plates, which echo the set of antique ceramic designs on the wall. Cut-glass candlesticks can be converted into lamps, such as the pair shown here.

With its high-gloss, faux-
tortoiseshell walls, tripartite mirror,
and black-shaded candlestick lamps,
this vanity niche designed by
Anouska Hempel is a dramatic
setting for the daily rite of dressing
up. The vintage traveling hat box
resting on the shelf makes a
handsome storage container.

88

The simplest table can be transformed into a romantic vanity by covering it with pieces of lace, as designer Laura Ashley has done here. Nineteenth-century fashion illustrations, readily available through antique dealers, are especially appropriate adornments for dressing tables.

HIDDEN TREASURES

STORAGE, STORAGE, STORAGE

The photographs in this chapter offer dozens of ways to solve one of the major problems you are likely to face when decorating the bedroom: creating storage space that is not only sufficient and convenient but also in keeping with the room's decor.

• *BEHIND CLOSED DOORS:* One basic approach to storage is to hide everything tidily behind the closed doors of closets, cabinets, and the like. The doors of these storage units themselves can be turned into decorative features. Mirror them to increase the sense of space in the room (page 102). Panel them (pages 100, 117), paper them, or cover them with fabric (page 92). Hang paintings, prints, or photographs on them (pages 101, 117). If you don't have built-in closets, an inexpensive alternative is to curtain off a portion of the room (pages 94, 95). Dressing tents, such as the Edwardian one on page 99, make delightfully stylish portable closets.

• *SHOWING OFF:* The other approach to storage is to keep stored items in full or partial view so that their colors and textures can become part of the decor. Open shelves (page 120), glass-fronted cabinets (page 97), and cabinet or closet doors with decorative cut-out patterns (page 103) are just some of the ways to achieve this effect.

• *FOUND OBJECTS:* If your budget does not permit the purchase of such traditional storage units as armoires (page 98), bureaus, or chests of drawers, you can find all sorts of inexpensive objects that make excellent repositories for clothes, shoes, linens, and many of the other items commonly stored in the bedroom. Vintage trunks (page 98), metal trunks (page 96), plastic laundry baskets (page 96), and rattan baskets (page 104) can all serve as the basic components of imaginative storage systems. Hat boxes (pages 94, 129), shoe boxes (page 96), and even sturdy shopping bags (page 81) are ideal for stashing away trinkets and odds and ends.

• *UNDER THE BED:* The dead space beneath the bed is perfect for storage. Boxes full of linens, clothes, or shoes can be stowed there. Custom-made drawers can be installed (page 101). Some contemporary platform beds are designed with built-in drawers.

92

PAGES 90 AND 91

Much of the charm of this early-nineteenth-century New England stenciled bedroom, now in the American Museum in Britain, lies in the bandboxes of different sizes, each covered in a delightful patterned paper of the period. These decorative storage containers can be easily and inexpensively approximated today by covering hat boxes and shoe boxes with decoratively printed wallpaper.

In this London bedroom designed by Sally Metcalfe of George Spencer, sliding closet doors have been imaginatively integrated into the decor by covering them with antique paisley shawls. (LEFT)

Fitted travel cases make convenient storage units for toiletries,
at home as well as on the road. (BELOW)

A wall of closets and cupboards keeps the clutter of worldly possessions tidily
out of sight, except for a few ties that provide a splash of color. (ABOVE)

94

A vintage chest whose glory has faded can be given new life with paint. In this room designed by John Stefanidis, a cotton curtain hung from a wooden rod adds a touch of softness to the wall behind the bed and a small painted chest. (ABOVE)

Ready-made curtains, flat sheets, and even shower curtains can be used to conceal clothes racks in a decorative way, as designers Osborne and Little have done here. Other everyday objects that can be pressed into service as storage units are shoe boxes and hat boxes, whether left as they are or turned into decorative objects by painting them or covering them with anything from wrapping paper to wallpaper. (LEFT)

The simplest, most economical way to create entire walls of closets is to install curtain rods all around the room and hang sheets from them. Designer Andrea de Montal has hidden the rods behind a wooden cornice, which she has painted white and adorned with festive ceramic plates, in keeping with the rustic charm of the painted country bed.

95

In the dressing area of this London artist's studio, a stack of ordinary plastic laundry baskets filled with freshly ironed shirts forms an inexpensive but chic storage system. Handkerchiefs and linen towels are tied with ribbons to prevent wrinkling, and shoes are stored in a pile of navy-blue boxes covered with tiny gold fleurs-de-lis. The artist's favorite Horst photograph lends a touch of class. (BELOW)

96

Utilitarian metal trunks, stacked under the staircase in a converted loft, add a bit of high-tech style while providing inexpensive storage space that can be moved when necessary. (ABOVE)

These glass-fronted cabinets, designed by architect William Monaghan for his New York loft, make it easy to locate a particular article of clothing at a glance. And the colors and textures of the garments contribute to the decor of the bedroom.

97

The doors of Fanny Ward's rustic painted armoire open to reveal striped, checked, and lacy white linens, towels, and pillows neatly organized in appealing piles. (ABOVE)

An antique Louis Vuitton steamer trunk, a distressed pine country cupboard, and several woven baskets provide ample storage that is in keeping with the spare, clean style of this airy California bedroom designed by Dot Spikings. (LEFT)

The fabric-covered Edwardian
dressing tent in Cecilia McEwen's
bedroom is now used as a closet that
is both decorative and portable.

99

The look of the handsome paneled doors in this bedroom designed by Sally Metcalfe of George Spencer can be approximated by adding strips of picture-frame molding to plain doors, or by painting illusionistic panels on them.

100

In historic Battersea House in London, an imposing portrait has wittily been incorporated into a pair of closet doors. You might not want to try this with a valuable painting: a large poster or trompe l'oeil mural would have much the same effect. (LEFT)

For some people the area under the bed is a dead space that only collects dust. But not for London designer and antiques dealer André de Cacqueray, who has added reproduction drawers underneath the frame of his majestic Empire bed. Freshly ironed monogrammed sheets are always within easy reach when it's time to change the bed. (BELOW)

101

102

The space-increasing effect of mirrored closet doors, like these designed by Monika Apponyi, can be achieved simply and inexpensively by attaching standard mirror panels to the doors and applying strip molding around them.

In this London flat designed by Trügelmann, drawers and shelves have been installed behind closet doors to maximize storage efficiency and minimize clutter. (BELOW)

103

Designer Christophe Gollut has added a touch of Gothic style to Baldassare La Rizza's wall of cupboards by replacing one opaque panel with a "window"—ornamented with delicate tracery—that permits a glimpse of the shirts behind. (ABOVE)

104

By lining the closet doors of her London bedroom with a Napoleonic bee-patterned fabric, Stephanie Hoppen has turned them into a decorative feature. The sets of antique linen tied with pale green ribbons show that even organization can have style. (ABOVE)

Richard Mudditt created this imaginative, efficient, and attractive storage unit by building shelves for ready-made rectangular baskets with cut-out handles to facilitate sliding them in and out. An alternative is to place the baskets on sliding trays or in drawer frames. Leave the baskets plain for a natural look or paint them to complement the rest of the room's decor. (LEFT)

Fashion designer Bill Blass's dressing room is a study in the aesthetics of storage. The soft hues of the row of suits echo the tones of the collection of pictures on the walls. The fine neoclassical dresser provides both additional storage space and sophistication. Note the banked shelf for shoes. If you don't have a separate dressing room, you might consider converting a corner of your bedroom into a dressing area.

105

PERFECT UNIONS

BEDDING DOWN IN OTHER ROOMS

Today more and more people are living in one-room spaces, whether by choice or from necessity, and the bed must therefore coexist with all the other furniture in the space. The following pages provide many examples of happy marriages between the bed and the all-in-one room.

• VERSATILE BEDS: Beds that convert into seating or that can be folded up and put away in a closet or cabinet offer the greatest flexibility. Sofa beds, trundle beds (page 112), futons, and high risers all function as comfortable beds when open and as space-saving, attractive seating when closed. Murphy beds, which retract into a special compartment built into the wall, and beds that can be hidden in a closet or armoire (page 108) leave no indication that the room is used for sleeping as soon as they are put away. If space permits a large bed, you may want to dress it as a sofa rather than as a bed, so that guests will naturally gravitate toward it for seating. The bed with

upholstered frame in fashion designer Bill Blass's library is an example (pages 118–19). You need not "camouflage" the bed at all, of course, and it can occupy a corner of the room or be the center of attention (pages 109, 111).

• SLEEPING LOFTS: If your ceiling is high enough, you might consider constructing a sleeping loft above the main living area, thereby gaining both privacy and additional space. A staircase or even a simple ladder provides easy access (page 113).

• PARTITIONING THE ROOM: There are many ways to give architectural definition to the sleeping area in a one-room living space. Raising the bed on a platform, for instance, emphasizes its importance (page 114). Columns can be used to define a space that sets the bed apart in its own "room" (pages 114–15). Inherently decorative folding screens conceal the bed from view and can be moved around at whim (page 114).

PAGES 106 AND 107

Part bedroom, part study, and part informal dining room, this versatile space, designed by the late Laura Ashley, unites diverse patterns and textures through its red, gold, and black color scheme.

When dinner is over in this London flat designed by André de Cacqueray, table and chairs are pushed aside, an antique armoire is opened, and the bed that resides within is opened. No detail has been overlooked: reading lights have been installed in the top of the armoire and its interior has been lined with fabric. (ABOVE AND LEFT)

In artist Julian Barrow's London studio a fancifully shaped Regency campaign bed has pride of place in front of the fire. The painting on the easel behind the bed is a copy by Barrow of John Singer Sargent's portrait of Robert Louis Stevenson. Sargent once occupied a studio in the same building.

109

110

Libraries, like bedrooms, are designed for comfort, and combining the two, as designer Christophe Gollut has done here, can result in an exceptionally warm, cozy refuge. The bed faces the focal point of the room, an exquisitely carved chimneypiece with Corinthian pilasters and an inset overmantel mirror. The deep, rich red of the wood is picked up in the bedspread and in the fabric covering the walls. (LEFT)

A provincial sleigh bed, country table and chairs, and faux-bamboo rocking chair lend a rustic feeling to the sleeping and dining areas of this open, minimalist space designed by Port of Call. A fluted column base serves as an imaginative bedside table. (FACING PAGE)

In a diminutive one-room flat in London, designed by Roger Banks-Pye of Colefax and Fowler, an elegant, Regency-inspired trundle bed serves as attractive seating by day and opens into a comfortable double bed at night. Linens are stored in a roomy, chest-shaped rattan basket.
(ABOVE AND LEFT)

An open sleeping loft built over the living room in this California house designed by Dot Spikings maximizes the use of space without impeding the influx of light. A no-frills ladder leads to this airy aerie.

113

In this London loft, the sleeping, dining, and living areas are defined by columns and by the placement of the furniture. The diamond motif that is carved into the columns, cornices, and baseboards gives a stylistic unity to the whole space. With its strong, straight lines and characteristic slats, the Mission furniture echoes the ceiling beams. A decorative wooden screen provides privacy when needed for the sleeping area. (FACING PAGE AND RIGHT)

Furnished with faux-bamboo
daybeds, a guest bedroom in Anna
Fendi's Roman house doubles as a
sitting room. The soft, paisley-
patterned wall covering, pillows,
and upholstery give the room a cozy
intimacy, while the painted coved
ceiling lends it architectural interest.

116

In this bedroom designed by David Hicks, one can literally roll out of bed into a steaming-hot bath. The stonelike flooring complements both the floral-printed canopy hangings and the granitelike facing of the porcelain tub. (RIGHT)

This grandly paneled room may not appear at first glance able to accommodate guests, but one of the panels is actually a door to a closet that has been transformed into a sleeping alcove. (BELOW)

117

With its upholstered frame and
headboard, the bed in fashion
designer Bill Blass's library-bedroom
looks like, and doubles as, a sofa.
(FACING PAGE AND RIGHT)

A platform built into a niche transforms this tiny space, designed by Stickland Coombe Architecture, into a sunny, inviting bedroom, complete with its own washstand and convenient shelving for linens and towels.

A nineteenth-century metal bed has pride of place in artist Jeff Leckie's New York studio, which serves as bedroom, workroom, dining room, and living room. The handsome paneled-look wall treatment can be easily and inexpensively achieved with strips of molding. The skylight not only is an excellent source of light but also gives the room a welcome sense of spaciousness.

121

1,001 NIGHTS

BEDROOMS THAT DREAMS ARE MADE OF

"The romantic mood is a point of view, . . . a secret world . . . so fully imagined by its author and so deeply realized that it becomes seductively real . . . an inner world where . . . you may dream the possible dream: that the wondrous is real, because that is how you feel it to be, that is how you wish it to be, . . . and how you wish it into being."

Diana Vreeland, D.V.

The bedroom is such a private place that you can let your imagination go and, using paint, architectural elements, wallpaper, fabric, furniture, and decorative props, realize your wildest fantasy. Whether your dream bedroom is as basic as a hammock slung across a porch (page 134) or as exotic as a maharajah's sleeping quarters, fantasy is about making the inaccessible accessible, about bringing "into being" a world that is not part of your daily life.

• SOURCES OF INSPIRATION: Styles of the past, faraway places you've visited, paintings, photographs, books, and even films can all serve as sources of inspiration for the bedroom of your dreams. For instance, if you've always been drawn to Henri Matisse's color-splashed canvases of the south of France or of seductively reclining odalisques in settings ablaze with vibrant patterns, you might consider painting walls, floors, and furniture in vivid colors and ornamental motifs. Or, if your most romantic vacation spot was a thatched hut on an island in the Indian Ocean (pages 132–33), why not transform that cherished memory into a lifelong reality by covering the walls, floors, and windows of your bedroom with inexpensive natural-fiber matting, draping mosquito netting from the ceiling, and dressing the bed in native cotton fabric?

• A SENSE OF STYLE: As different as the bedrooms shown in this book are, they all share one thing in common— a strong, individual sense of style. No matter what your source of inspiration may be, your personal interpretation of it is what will give the room its character. The beauty of fantasy is that you need not follow anyone's rules but your own. Lillian Williams's bedroom, for example, takes its inspiration from eighteenth-century France, but she has infused it with her own vision of the period, such as the charming display of hat boxes and antique shoes; the result is a unique decorative statement (pages 128–29). So, when designing your bedroom, let your dreams be your guide.

PAGES 122 AND 123

Dressing a hammock or bed in brightly colored Kenyan fabrics can capture a bit of the exotic pleasure of dozing in a hammock strung across a dhow as it drifts lazily along the coast of Kenya.

If you hanker for a bedroom fit for a pasha, let the one in this Turkish yali, or painted wooden house, be your inspiration. Its gilded furniture, coffered ceiling, and traces of a delicately painted frieze and cornice are all elements that can be adapted without spending a fortune. For instance, you could paint the design of the bed's elaborately carved ornamentation right on the wall.

(RIGHT)

124

An intricately carved and painted wooden bed
dictates the decor of this room in an Istanbul house.
A pair of tree-trunk columns defines the entrance
to the room, and a white balustrade separates it
from the adjoining room, creating a sense of
architectural division without walls.

125

A guest bedroom at Drumlanrig, Scotland, is nothing short of a dream come true. The enchanting effect of its tapestry-covered walls can be achieved by hanging period or reproduction wallpaper panels on the walls or by painting your own panoramic scenes.

126

Exuberantly carved, painted, and gilded furniture lends a fairy-tale atmosphere to this bedroom in a Swiss chalet.

127

Stepping into Lillian Williams's
New York bedroom is like entering
a boudoir in an eighteenth-century
French château or folly. The period
feel is captured in the painted
paneling, antique textiles, sconces,
profusion of candles, and the framed
fashion prints hung from ribbons
on the walls.

128

Every object in the room enhances its eighteenth-century aesthetic, from the collection of chests to the vintage shoes to the fabric ribbons. (BELOW)

Hat boxes covered in decorative paper serve as storage containers and also contribute to the eighteenth-century French charm of Lillian Williams's bedroom.
(ABOVE AND RIGHT)

Fabric designer Jim Thompson
created his fantasy bedroom in
Bangkok. The furnishings are culled
from traditional Thai houses, and
the silks covering the bed and
pillows beautifully complement
the fine collection of Oriental
pictures that adorns the walls.
A collection of artwork or objects
can be the impetus for creating
your own fantasy bedroom, no
matter where you live.

130

Traveling in such homey comfort may only be wishful thinking today, but this Victorian caravan, or sleeping car, is filled with ideas for re-creating the quaintness of a bygone era in your own bedroom. Delicately painted designs turn walls, moldings, and ceilings into decorative features. The bed is housed in a cozy niche atop built-in storage cupboards. And the brightly colored carpet, hand-crocheted afghan, and pillows are counterbalanced by the lacy curtains and tablecloth and the etched-glass gas lamps and door panes.

(RIGHT AND BELOW)

131

132

For most of us, a thatched-roof cottage by the sea is an exotic reverie. But on the island of Lamu near the coast of Kenya it is a way of life. Natural-fiber matting covers the walls and floors of the bedroom, and window shades of the same material can be rolled down for privacy. The ceiling is tented with mosquito netting, and the bedspreads and curtains are made out of a brightly patterned native fabric. (LEFT)

The bedroom looks out on the open porch, where cane plantation chairs and a hammock promise respite from the tropical sun. (FACING PAGE)

A hammock strung from two posts or two trees, whether in a tropical paradise or in your own backyard, makes the most idyllic bedroom of them all. (FACING PAGE AND RIGHT)

SOURCES

UNITED STATES

Department-Store/ General Furnishings and Accessories Chains

Bloomingdale's
Bullock's
Crate & Barrel
Dillard's
Ikea
Macy's
Neiman-Marcus
Pottery Barn
Saks Fifth Avenue
Stein Mart

Mail Order

L. L. Bean
Freeport, ME 04033
(800) 221-4221

Chambers
P.O. Box 7841
San Francisco, CA 94120
(800) 334-9790

The Company Store
500 Company Store Road
La Crosse, WI 54601-4477
Tel: (800) 323-8000

Crate & Barrel
P.O. Box 9059
Wheeling, IL 60090
(800) 323-5461
(708) 520-4747

Cuddledown of Maine
312 Canco Road
Portland, ME 04101
(800) 323-6793

Eddie Bauer
P.O. Box 3700
Seattle, WA 98124
(800) 426-8020

Ellenburg's Wicker & Casual
P. O. Box 5638
Statesville, NC 28687
(800) 841-1420
(704) 873-2900

Garnet Hill
262 Main Street
Franconia, NH 03580
(800) 622-6216
(603) 823-5545

Hammacher Schlemmer
9180 Le Saint Drive
Fairfield, OH 45014
(800) 543-3366
(513) 860-4570

Heavenly Down
7245 Whipple Avenue
North Canton, OH 44720
(800) 898-3696
(216) 494-2323

Hold Everything
Mail Order Department
P.O. Box 7807
San Francisco, CA 94120-7807
(800) 421-2264

The Horchow Collection
P.O. Box 620048
Dallas, TX 75262-0048
(800) 456-7000
(214) 556-6000

Land's End "Coming Home" Catalogue
1 Land's End Lane
Dept. FW
Dodgeville, WI 53595
(800) 356-4444

Paper White
P.O. Box 956
Fairfax, CA 94930
(800) 677-1991

Pottery Barn
100 North Point Street
San Francisco, CA 94133
(800) 922-5507

Shaker Workshop
P.O. Box 1028
Concord, MA 01742
(800) 840-9121
(517) 646-8985

Telephone Order

Dial-a-Mattress
1-800-MATTRES

NEW YORK

Department/General Furnishings and Accessories Stores

ABC Carpet & Home
888 Broadway

Barney's
660 Madison Avenue

Bed, Bath and Beyond
620 Avenue of the Americas

Bergdorf Goodman
745 Fifth Avenue

Felissimo
10 West 56th Street

Laura Ashley Home Furnishings
714 Madison Avenue

Laytner's Country Furniture
2270 Broadway

Portico Collection
379 West Broadway

Zona
97 Greene Street

Beds

Arise Futon
415 Amsterdam Avenue;
17 East Fourth Street;
265 West 72nd Street

Barton-Sharpe Ltd.
119 Spring Street

Daniel Mack Rustic Furnishing
11 West 19th Street

Door Store
1 Park Avenue;
1201 Third Avenue;
123 West 17th Street

Antiques/Furnishings/ Accessories

Alice's Antiques
505 Columbus Avenue

Charlotte Moss
1027 Lexington Avenue

Chartreuse
309 East 9th Street

Cobweb Antique Imports
116 West Houston Street

De Lorenzo
958 Madison Avenue

Evergreen Antiques
1249 Third Avenue

Five Eggs
436 West Broadway

Frederick P. Victoria & Son
154 East 55th Street

Hands All Around
986 Madison Avenue

Howard Kaplan Antiques
827 Broadway

Judith Amdur
1193 Lexington Avenue

Kentshire Galleries, Ltd.
37 East 12th Street

Linda Horn Antiques
1015 Madison Avenue

Newel Art Galleries
425 East 53rd Street

Niall Smith Antiques and Decorations
344B Bleecker Street;
96 Grand Street

Pamela Scurry's Wicker Garden
1318 Madison Avenue

Paris Apartment
324 and 328 East Ninth Street

Pierre Deux
870 Madison Avenue

Pimlico Way
1028 Lexington Avenue

Juan Portela
138 East 71st Street

Ralph Lauren Home Collection
867 Madison Avenue

Slatkin & Co.
131 East 70th Street

William Wayne & Co.
846–850 Lexington Avenue

Linens/Bedclothes

Ad Hoc Softwares
410 West Broadway

E. Braun & Co.
717 Madison Avenue

Descamps
723 Madison Avenue

The Down Quilt Shop
518 Columbus Avenue

Frette Linen
799 Madison Avenue

The Gazebo
127 East 57th Street

Leron, Inc. Linen
750 Madison Avenue

D. Porthault & Co.
18 East 69th Street

Portico Bed and Bath
139 Spring Street

Pratesi Linens
829 Madison Avenue

Schweitzer Linens
457 Columbus Avenue;
1132 Madison Avenue;
1053 Lexington Avenue

Wolfman, Gold & Good
116 Greene Street

*Antique Linens/
Textiles/Bedclothes*

America Hurrah
766 Madison Avenue

Ann Jacob America
Antiques
756 Madison Avenue

Hope & Wilder
454 Broome Street

Laura Fisher Antiques
390 Bleecker Street

Susan Parrish Antiques
390 Bleecker Street

Thomas K. Woodard
799 Madison Avenue

Trouvaille Française
552 East 87th Street
(By appt.)

Antiques Markets

The Annex Antiques Fair
& Flea Market
Sixth Avenue from 24th to
28th Street

Manhattan Arts and
Antiques Center
1050 Second Avenue

OTHER U.S. CITIES

Abodio
5961 Corson Avenue South
Seattle, WA 98108

Amethyst
5514 Germantown Avenue
Philadelphia, PA 19144

Annabelle's
5017 West 119th Street
Overland Park, KS 66209

The Arrangement
4210 NE Fremont
Portland, OR 97213

The Bath and Linen Shoppe
2058 San Marco
Jacksonville, FL 32207

Eddie Bauer Home
Collection Retail
3770 150th Avenue NE
Redmond, WA 98052

Bedfellows
3425 Thomasville Road
Carriage Gate Center
Tallahassee, FL 32308

Bedspread and Linen
House
17311 135th Avenue NE,
#B-100
Woodinville, WA 98072

Benchmark Design Center
1-35 and 87th Street
Lenexa, KS 66212

Bennett Galleries
4515 Kingston Pike
Knoxville, TN 37919

Blackwelders Furniture
12475 South Dixie
Highway
Miami, FL 33156

The Bon
Third and Pine Street
Seattle, WA 98181

Bonnin Ashley
Antiques, Inc.
4707 SW 72nd Avenue
Miami, FL 33155

The Cadeau
2316 Guadalupe
Austin, TX 78705

The Complete B&B
615 NW 23rd
Portland, OR 97210

Contemporary Home
Furnishings
8977 Metcalf
Overland Park, KS 66212

Cottage Interiors
P.O. Box 1187
Poulsbo, WA 98370

Country Furnishing
2005 5th Avenue
Seattle, WA 98121

Curtain Shop
Hogan Road
Bangor, ME 04401;
Shaw's Plaza
Waterville, ME 04901

Daisy Kingdom
134 NW Eighth
Portland, OR 97209

David's Home Fashions
3480 Plaza Avenue
Memphis, TN 38111

Davis Bedroom Gallery
1033 Chestnut Street
Philadelphia, PA 19107

Details
4079 Calder Avenue
Beaumont, TX 77706

Domaine
661 120th Avenue NE
Bellevue, WA 98005

Domus
141 Bellevue Square
Bellevue, WA 98004

Feathered Friends
1419 First Avenue
Seattle, WA 98101

Festivities
9701 15th Avenue NW
Seattle, WA 98117

Fine-Line Furniture
and Accessories
1210 South Dixie Highway
Coral Gables, FL 33146

Fine Lines
2712 West 53rd Street
Mission, KS 66205

Fuhr's Interiors
12800 Shawnee Mission
Parkway
Shawnee, KS 66216

Golden Bed Antiques
343 South Street
Philadelphia, PA 19147

Greenstreet Interiors
4046 Belleview
Kansas City, MO 64112

Habitat
3801 Old Seward
Highway, #5
Anchorage, AK 99503

Homestead
223 East Main
Fredericksburg, TX 78624

Hot Pots
Marketplace at Salishon
Gleneden Beach, OR
97388

In the Beginning Quilts
8201 Lake City Way NE
Seattle, WA 98115

Virginia Jacobs
2328 NW Westover
Portland, OR 97210

Kasala
1505 Western Avenue
Seattle, WA 98101

Keegs
310 Broadway East
Seattle, WA 98102

Kitchen Kaboodle
3219 NW Guam
Portland, OR 97210

Pierre Lafond
516 San Ysidro
Santa Barbara, CA 93108

Langley Market and
Mercantile
P.O. Box 307
Langley, WA 98260

Legacy Linens
7406 Brookhaven Circle
Memphis, TN 38117

Linen Store
4055 Hillsboro Road
Nashville, TN 37215

Linens and Things
9034 Metcalf
Overland Park, KS 66212

Linens Etc.
20929 Ventura Boulevard
Woodland Hills, CA 91364

Lucky's Antique Gallery
and Fine Reproductions
9480 South Dixie Highway
Miami, FL 33156

Luxe
5828 Sunset Drive
Miami, FL 33143

Made in France
301 West End Avenue
Nashville, TN 37203

Meier and Frank
621 SW Fifth
Portland, OR 97204

Metro Home Furnishings
570 East Benson Avenue
Anchorage, AK 99503

Miller Pollard
4741 University Village
Plaza NE
Seattle, WA 98105

Molbaks
13625 NE 175th Avenue
Woodinville, WA 98072

Niktex Bed and Bath
154 Bellevue Square Mall
Bellevue, WA 98004

Nordstrom-Boardwalk
1501 5th Avenue
Seattle, WA 98101

Now and Then Collectibles
4832 SW 72nd Avenue
Miami, FL 33155

Nu-D-Zine Bedding
and Bath
1006 Lincoln Road
Miami Beach, FL 33139

Osman's Furniture
15205 Metcalf
South Overland Park, KS
66223

Pacific Linen
2222 220th SE, #200
Bothell, WA 98021

Pioneer Linens Co.
210-212 Clematis Street
West Palm Beach, FL
33402

L Pizitz
County Road, #30-A
Seaside, Fl 32459

Plantation Shop
4828 First Coast Highway
Amelia Island, FL 32034

Propper Bros.
4368 Cressmont Street
Philadelphia, PA 19127

137

Quilt Ladies
4266 Manayunk Avenue
Philadelphia, PA 19127

Rafie Corporation
(Bed and Bath)
3000 184th Street SW
Lynwood, WA 98037

Molly Reed
30 North Central Avenue
Medford, OR 97501

Reverie
7615 West Farmington
Boulevard
Germantown, TN 38137

Ron Robinson
d.b.a. Fred Segal
8066 Melrose Avenue, #3
Los Angeles, CA 90046

Rooms Unlimited
11087 Frontage Road
Kenai, AK 99611

Room with a View
1600 Montana Avenue
Santa Monica, CA 90403

Ron Ross/Elizabeth Tilkian
12950 Ventura Boulevard
Toluca Lake, CA 91602

Salish Lodge
P.O. Box 1109
Snoqualmie, WA 98065

Scandia Down
215 West 47th Street
Kansas City, MO 64112

Somnia
117-21 Franklin Boulevard
Philadelphia, PA 19154;
4050 Main Street
Philadelphia, PA 19127

Spanglers
6927 Tomahawk Road
Prairie Village, KS 66208

Staircase
8645 Sunset Boulevard
Los Angeles, CA 90069

Surroundings
Main Street
Camden, ME 04843

Trivia
355 NW Gilman
Boulevard
St. Georges Square
Issaquah, WA 98027

Victoria's Armoire
4077 Ponce de Leon
Coral Gables, FL 33146

Jackson Weeks Interiors
342 Main Street
Franklin, TN 37064

GREAT BRITAIN

Mail-Order Catalogues

Antique Designs
Penny Kempton
Orchard Farm
Brow Lane
Antrobus
Cheshire
CW9 6JY
(0565) 777-376

Cologne & Cotton
74 Regent Street
Leamington Spa
Warwickshire CV32 4NS
(0926) 332-573

The Green Catalogue
Freepost SN2 901
Chippenham
Wiltshire SN14 6QZ
(0249) 444-663

Melin Tregwynt
Castle Morris
Haverford West
Pembrokeshire
(0138) 891-644

The White Company
298-300 Munster Road
London SW6
(0171) 385-7988

LONDON AND ENVIRONS

Department/General Furnishings and Accessories Stores

The Conran Shop
The Michelin Building
81 Fulham Road, SW3

General Trading Company
144 Sloane Street, SW1

Graham & Green
4 Elgin Crescent, W11

Habitat
196 Tottenham Court
Road, W1;
206 King's Road, SW3

Harrod's
Knightsbridge, SW1

Harvey Nichols
109-125 Knightsbridge,
SW1

Heal's
196 Tottenham Court
Road, W1

Ikea
2 Drury Way
North Circular Road,
NW10

Jerry's Home Store
163-167 Fulham Road,
SW3

Laura Ashley
256 Regent Street, W1

John Lewis
278-306 Oxford Street,
W1

Liberty
Regent Street, W1

Muji, No Brand Goods
26 Great Marlborough
Street, W1;
157 Kensington High
Street, W8

Peter Jones
Sloane Square, SW1

Selfridges
400 Oxford Street, W1

Beds

Alphabeds
92 Tottenham Court
Road, W1

And So To Bed
636 King's Road, SW6

Artisan
797 Wandsworth Road,
SW8

Grange
Harrod's
Knightsbridge, SW1

Renwick and Clarke
Trading
535 King's Road, SW10

Shaker Shop
25 Harcourt Street, W1;
322 King's Road, SW3

Space
28 All Saints' Road, W1

Antique Beds

A Barn Full of Brass Beds
Abbey House
Eastfield Road
Louth
Lincolnshire LN11 7HJ

After Noah
121 Upper Street, N1

Bed Bazaar
The Old Station
Station Road
Framlingham
Woodbridge
Suffolk IP13 9EE

André de Cacqueray
227 Ebury Street, SW1

Rupert Cavendish
610 King's Road, SW6

Christopher Gibbs
8 Vigo Street, W1

Judy Greenwood Antiques
657 Fulham Road, SW6

Guinevere Antiques Ltd.
578 King's Road, SW6

Simon Horn Furniture
117-121 Wandsworth
Bridge Road, SW6

H.R.W. Antiques
4a King's Avenue, SW4

William Sheppee
1A Church Avenue, SW14

Somerset House of Iron
779 Fulham Road, SW6

Universal Providers
86 Golborne Road, W10

Built-in Beds

The London Wall Bed
Company
263 The Vale, W3

Smallbone & Co.
(Devizes) Ltd.
105 Fulham Road, SW3

Linens/Bedclothes

Elizabeth Baer
Pavilion Antiques
Freshford Hall
Freshford
Nr. Bath
Avon BA3 6EJ

Claridge & Co.
154 Wandsworth Bridge
Road, SW6

Country Road
151 Fulham Road, SW7

Damask
3-4 Broxholme House
New King's Road, SW6

J&M Davidson
62 Ledbury Road, W11

Descamps
197 Sloane Street, SW1

Frette
98 New Bond Street, W1

Givan's Irish Linen Store
207 King's Road, SW3

Irish Linen Co.
35 Burlington Arcade, W1

The Linen Merchant
11 Montpelier Street, SW7

The Monogrammed Linen
Shop
168 Walton Street, SW3

Le Tissus Français
227 Ebury Street, SW1

The White House
51/52 New Bond Street, W1

Antique Linens/Textiles

The Gallery of Antique
Costume and Textiles
2 Church Street, NW8

Marilyn Garrow Antique
Textiles
6 The Broadway, SW13

Lunn Antiques
86 New King's Road, SW6

Christopher Moore
Textiles
1 Munro Terrace
Cheyne Walk, SW10

Museum Quilts
254 Goswell Road, EC1

Peta Smyth Antiques
42 Moreton Street, SW1

*Antiques/Furniture/
Fabric/Accessories*

The Blue Door
77 Church Road, SW13

Maryse Boxer and
Carolyn Quartermaine
Chez Joseph
26 Sloane Street, SW1

Nina Campbell
9 Walton Street, SW3

Jane Churchill
151 Sloane Street, SW1

Colefax and Fowler
39 Brook Street, W1;
110 Fulham Road, SW3

Thomas Dare
341 King's Road, SW3

Designers Guild
267 & 277 King's Road,
SW3

Egg
36 Kinnerton Street, SW1

Pierre Frey
253 Fulham Road, SW3

Garouste & Bonetti/
David Gill Gallery
60 Fulham Road, SW3

Christophe Gollut
116 Fulham Road, SW3

Nicholas Haslam
12 Holbein Place, SW1

Ralph Lauren Home
Collection at Harvey
Nichols
109-125 Knightsbridge,
SW1

Les Olivades
7 Walton Street, SW3

David Linley Furniture,
Ltd.
60 Pimlico Road, SW1

Mrs. Monro
16 Motcomb Street, SW1

Mulberry At Home
at Harvey Nichols
109-125 Knightsbridge,
SW1

Osborne and Little
304 King's Road, SW3

Port of Call, Ltd.
13 Walton Street, SW3

Souleiado
171 Fulham Road, SW3

George Spencer
Designs Ltd.
4 West Halkin Street, SW1

John Stefanidis
261 Fulham Road, SW3

The Study
41 Shad Thames, SE1

Tobias and the Angel
66–68 White Hart Lane,
SW13

Timney-Fowler
388 King's Road, SW3

Valerie Wade
108 Fulham Road, SW3

Joanna Wood Ltd.
48A Pimlico Road, SW3

William Yeoward
336 King's Road, SW3

*Made-to-Order
Headboards*

The Dormy House
Stirling Park
East Portway Industrial
Estate
Andover
Hants SP10 3TZ

Highfields Headboards
Highfields Farm
Grove Hill
Pembroke
SA71 5PU

Mosquito Netting

Trailfinders Travel
Goods Shop
50 Earl's Court Road, W8

*Trimmings/Tassels/
Hardware*

Wendy Cushing
Unit M7
Chelsea Garden Market
Chelsea Harbour, SW10

WH Newson
61 Pimlico Road, SW1

VV Rouleaux, Ltd.
Ribbons, Trimmings,
and Braids
10 Symons Street, SW3

Wallpaper

Baer & Ingram Wallpapers
273 Wandsworth Bridge
Road, SW6

Zuber
42 Pimlico Road, SW1

*Open-Air Antiques
Markets*

Bermondsey
Bermondsey Square and
Tower Bridge Road, SE1

Camden Passage
Islington, N1

Portobello Road, W11

Indoor Antiques Markets

Antiquarius Antique
Market
131 King's Road, SW3

Chenil Galleries
181-183 King's Road, SW3

Gray's Antique Market
58 Davies Street, W1

Prints/Pictures

Norman Blackburn
32 Ledbury Road, W11

Julia Boston
14 Wilby Mews, W11

Stephanie Hoppen
Decorative Pictures
17 Walton Street, SW3

Print Rooms

Nicola Wingate-Saul
Print Rooms
43 Moreton Street, SW1

Salvage

Architectural Salvage
Register (Index of salvage
dealers and items)
(0483) 203-221

Crowthers of Syon
Lodge Ltd.
Syon Lodge
Busch Corner
London Road
Isleworth, Middlesex,
TW7 5BH

LassCo Architectural
Antique Salvage
Mark Street
(off Paul Street)
London EC2

Walcot Reclamation
108 Walcot Street
Bath
Avon BA1 5BG

FRANCE

PARIS

*Department/General
Furnishings and
Accessories Stores*

BHV
52 rue de Rivoli, 75004

Le Bon Marché
22 rue de Sèvres, 75007

The Conran Shop
117 rue du Bac, 75007

Galeries Lafayette
40 bd Haussmann, 75009

Habitat
17 rue de l'Arrivée, 75014

Ikea
202 rue Henri Barbusse,
78370 Plaisir

Printemps Haussmann
64 bd Haussmann, 75009

Samaritaine
19 rue de la Monnaie,
75001

Linens/Bedclothes

La Boutique du Sommeil
24 avenue Pierre-ler-de-
Serbie, 75016

Carré Blanc
33 rue de Sèvres, 75006;
111 bis, rue de Courcelles,
75017

Casa Caïada
12 rue Jacob, 75006

La Chatelaine
170 av Victor Hugo, 75016

Chiff-Tir
20 av des Ternes, 75017

Agnès Comar S.A.
7 av Georges V, 75008

Yves Delorme
153 rue Saint-Honoré,
75001

Anaïk Descamps
at Galeries Lafayette
40 bd Haussmann, 75009

Boutique Descamps
44 rue de Passy, 75016;
38 rue du Four, 75006;
and branches

Descamps Michel Ange
Auteuil
4 rue Donizetti, 75016

Olivier Desforges
26 bd Raspail, 75007;
8 av Mozart, 75016

Christian Dior
32 av Montaigne, 75008

Frette
48 faubourg Saint-
Honoré, 75008

Muriel Grateau Boutique
Maison
132–133 galerie de Valois,
75001

Yves Halard
252 bis, bd Saint-
Germain, 75007

Kenzo
3 place des Victoires,
75001

La Maison de Renata
2 bd Raspail, 75007

Matins Bleus
92 rue de Rennes, 75006

Catherine Memmi
32-34 rue Saint-Sulpice,
75006

Nouez-Moi
27 rue des Sablons, 75016

Nuit Blanche
41 rue de Bourgogne,
75007

La Paresse en Douce
97 rue du Bac, 75007

Porthault
18 av Montaigne, 75008

Nina Ricci
39 av Montaigne, 75008

Le Trefle Bleu
2 rue Largillière, 75016

Furniture/Fabric/
Wallpaper/Accessories

Biggie Best
28 rue Saint-Sulpice,
75006;
9/11 rue des Lavandières
Sainte-Opportune, 75001

Boutique Elle
30 rue Saint-Sulpice, 75006

Braquenié
111 bd Beaumarchais,
75003

Manuel Canovas
5 place Furstenberg,
75006

Comoglio Paris
22 rue Jacob, 75006

Etamine
63 rue du Bac, 75007

Etamine "La Fenêtre"
2 rue Furstenberg, 75006

Etat de Siège
21 av de Friedland, 75008;
94 rue du Bac, 75007;
1 quai Conti, 75006

Patrick Frey
47 rue des Petits Champs,
75001;
5 rue Jacob, 75006

Garouste et Bonetti
through Galerie Neotu
25 rue du Renard, 75004

Laura Ashley
261 rue Saint-Honoré,
75001

Ralph Lauren Home
Collection
2 place de la Madeleine,
75008

Maison de Famille
29 rue Saint-Sulpice, 75006

Marie-Christine de la
Rochefoucauld
16 rue de l'Université,
75007

Mlinaric, Henry and
Zervudachi
54 galerie de Montpensier,
75001

Nobilis-Fontan
29 rue Bonaparte, 75006

Noblesse Oblige
27 bis, rue de Bellechasse,
75007

Souleiado
83 av Paul Doumer, 75016

Taco
3 rue Furstenberg, 75006

Françoise Thibault
1 rue de Bourbon le
Château, 75006

Antique Textiles

Michele Aragon
21 rue Jacob, 75006

Aux Fils du Temps
33 rue de Grenelle, 75007

Madame Paul Ollivary
1 rue Jacob, 75006

Panoramic Wallpaper

Zuber
5 bd des Filles du
Calvaire, 75003

Markets

Le Village Saint-Paul
rue Saint Paul, 75004

Le Village Suisse
54 av de la Motte Piquet,
75007

Les marchés aux puces:
Clignancourt; St.-Ouen;
Vanves; Montreuil

Marché Didot
Porte de Vanves

PROVENCE

Michel Biehn
7 av des Quatre-Otages
84800 L'Isle-Sur-la-Sorgue

Edith Mézard
Château de l'Ange
84220 Lumières

Les Olivades
28 rue Lafayette
13210 St.-Rémy-de-
Provence
and branches

Musée Souleiado
39 rue Proudhon
13150 Tarascon

Souleiado
2 av de la Résistance
13210 St. Rémy-de-
Provence
and branches

ITALY

Linens/Bedclothes

MILAN

Bassetti
Corso Garibaldi, 20

Frette
Via Visconti di Modrone
15;
Corso Buenos Aires 82;
Corso Vercelli 23/25;
Via Torino 42

Mirabello
Via Montebello (corner of
Via San Marco)

Pratesi
Via Montenapoleone 27/B

Sogaro
Corso di Porta Romana, 40

ROME

Frette
Viale Libia 192;
Via del Corso 381;
Via Nazionale 84

VENICE

Jesurum
Ponte Canonica 4310

Martinuzzi
San Marco, 67

PISTOIA

Pratesi S.p.A.–
Direct Factory Sales
Località Ponte Stella
51034 Pistoia

AUSTRALIA

Bed/Linen/
Furnishings Chains

Country Road Homewear
David Jones
Laura Ashley

Antiques/Linens/
Furnishings/Accessories

Abode
550 Chapel Street
South Yarra, Victoria
3141

Country by Design
58 Ourimbah Road
Mosman, New South
Wales 2088

Ozzie Mozzie Nets
and Bedlinen
678 Barrenjoey Road
North Avalon, New South
Wales 2107

Powder Blue
410 New South Head
Road
Double Bay 2028

Seddon & De Welles
529 Military Road
Mosman, New South
Wales 2088

SELECTED BIBLIOGRAPHY

Agius, Pauline. Introduction by Stephen Jones. *Ackermann's Regency Furniture and Interiors.* Marlborough: The Crowood Press, 1984.

Ariès, Philippe, and Georges Duby, general editors. *A History of Private Life: Vol. 3. Passions of the Renaissance.* Translated by Arthur Goldhammer. Cambridge, Mass.: The Belknap Press of Harvard University Press, 1989.

Barwick, Jo Ann, and Norma Skurka. *Scandinavian Country.* New York: Clarkson Potter, 1991.

Beard, Geoffrey. *Craftsmen and Interior Decoration in England, 1660–1820.* London: John Bartholomew and Son, 1981; London: Bloomsbury Books, 1986.

———. *The National Trust Book of the English House Interior.* London: Viking, 1990.

Beldegreen, Alecia. *The Bed.* New York: Stewart, Tabori & Chang, Ltd., 1991.

Brédif, Josette. *Classic Printed Textiles from France, 1760–1843, Toiles de Jouy.* Paris: Editions Adam Biro, 1989. London: Thames and Hudson, 1989.

Briggs, Asa. *Victorian Things.* London: B. T. Batsford, Ltd., 1988.

Campbell, Nina, and Caroline Seebohm. *Elsie de Wolfe: A Decorative Life.* New York: Panache Press, 1992.

Chambers, James. *The English House.* London: Methuen London, Ltd., 1985.

Chippendale, Thomas. *The Gentleman and Cabinet-Maker's Director.* Reprint of 3d ed., 1762. New York: Dover Publications, 1966.

Collard, Frances. *Regency Furniture.* Woodbridge, Suffolk, England: Antique Collectors' Club, 1985.

Cruickshank, Dan, and Neil Burton. *Life in the Georgian City.* London: Viking, 1990.

Davidson, Caroline. *Women's Worlds: The Art and Life of Mary Ellen Best, 1809–1891.* Foreword by Howard Rutkowski. New York: Crown Publishers, 1985.

De Bonneville, Françoise. Preface by Marc Porthault. Translated by Deke Dusinberre. *The Book of Fine Linen.* Paris: Flammarion, 1994.

Dickson, Elizabeth, ed., *The Englishwoman's Bedroom.* London: Chatto & Windus, The Hogarth Press, 1985.

Douglas, Mary T., and Baron Isherwood. *The World of Goods.* New York: Basic Books, 1979.

Du Prey, Pierre de la Ruffinière. *Sir John Soane.* London: Victoria and Albert Museum, 1985.

Edel, Leon, ed. *Henry James: Selected Letters.* Cambridge, Mass., and London: The Belknap Press of Harvard University Press, 1987.

Fowler, John, and John Cornforth. *English Decoration in the Eighteenth Century.* London: Barrie and Jenkins, 1986.

Garrett, Elisabeth Donaghy. *At Home: The American Family, 1750–1870.* New York: Harry N. Abrams, 1990.

Gere, Charlotte. *Nineteenth-Century Decoration: The Art of the Interior.* London: Weidenfeld and Nicolson, 1989.

Gilliam, Jan Kirsten, and Betty Crowe Leviner. *Furnishing Williamsburg's Historic Buildings.* Williamsburg, Va.: Colonial Williamsburg Foundation, 1991.

Girouard, Mark. *A Country House Companion.* New Haven and London: Yale University Press, 1987.

———. *Life in the English Country House.* New Haven and London: Yale University Press, 1978; Harmondsworth, Middlesex, England, and New York: Penguin Books, 1980.

Groth, Håkan. *Neoclassicism in the North: Swedish Furniture and Interiors, 1770–1800.* London: Thames and Hudson, 1990.

Harris, Eileen. *Going to Bed.* London: Her Majesty's Stationery Office, Victoria and Albert Museum publication, 1981.

Heal, Sir Ambrose. *London Furniture Makers 1660–1840.* London: Butler and Tanner, Ltd., 1988.

Hepplewhite, George. *The Cabinet-Maker and Upholsterer's Guide.* Introduction by Joseph Aronson. Reprint of 3d ed., 1794. New York: Dover Publications, 1969.

Jackson-Stops, Gervase, and James Pipkin. *The English Country House: A Grand Tour.* London: Weidenfeld and Nicolson, and The National Trust, 1985.

James, Henry. *The Portrait of a Lady.* Introduction by Geoffrey Moore. Notes by Patricia Crick. Harmondsworth, Middlesex, England: Penguin Books, 1987.

Johnson, Lorraine, and Gabrielle Townsend. *Osborne and Little: The Decorated Room.* Exeter, Devon: Webb and Bower, Ltd., 1988.

Jones, Chester. *Colefax and Fowler.* London: Barrie and Jenkins, 1989.

Juin, Hubert. *Le Lit.* Paris: Hachette, 1980.

Ladd, Mary-Sargent. *The French Woman's Bedroom.* New York: Doubleday, 1991.

Lewis, Lady Theresa, ed. *Extracts of the Journals and Correspondence of Miss Berry, 1783–1852.* Vols. 1–3. London: Longmans, Green and Co., 1865.

Lucie-Smith, Edward. *Furniture: A Concise History.* New York and Toronto: Oxford University Press, 1979.

McKendrick, Neil, John Brewer, and J. H. Plumb. *The Birth of a Consumer Society: The Commercialization of Eighteenth-Century England.* Bloomington: Indiana University Press, 1982.

Mitford, Mary Russell. *Our Village: Sketches of Rural Character and Scenery.* Vols. 1–2. Paris: Baudry's European Library, 1839.

Montgomery, Florence. *Textiles in America 1650–1870.* New York: W. W. Norton and Co., 1984.

Morley, John. *Regency Design 1790–1840.* London: A. Zwemmer, Ltd., 1793.

Morris, Christopher, ed. *The Journeys of Celia Fiennes.* London: The Cresset Press, Ltd., 1947.

Mott, George, and Sally Sample Aall. *Follies and Pleasure Pavilions.* Introduction by Gervase Jackson-Stops. London: Pavilion Books, 1989.

Nylander, Richard C., Elizabeth Redmond, and Penny J. Sander. *Wallpaper in New England.* Boston: Society for the Preservation of New England Antiquities, 1986.

Parissien, Steven. *Adam Style.* London: Phaidon Press, 1992.

———. *Regency Style.* London: Phaidon Press, 1992.

Praz, Mario. *An Illustrated History of Interior Decoration from Pompeii to Art Nouveau.* London: Thames and Hudson, 1964.

Rêves D'Alcôves: La Chambre au Cours des Siècles. Paris: Union Centrale des Arts Décoratifs—Réunion des Musées Nationaux, 1995.

Rosomon, Treve. *London Wallpapers: Their Manufacture and Use, 1690–1840.* London: English Heritage, 1992.

Rothstein, Natalie. *Silk Designs of the Eighteenth Century in the Collection of the Victoria and Albert Museum.* London: Thames and Hudson and the Board of Trustees of the Victoria and Albert Museum, 1990.

Rybczynski, Witold. *Home: A Short History of an Idea.* New York: Viking Penguin, 1986.

Saumarez Smith, Charles. *Eighteenth-Century Decoration: Design and the Domestic Interior in England.* London: Weidenfeld and Nicolson, 1993.

Schama, Simon. *The Embarrassment of Riches: An Interpretation of Dutch Culture in the Golden Age.* New York: Alfred A. Knopf, 1987.

Sheraton, Thomas. *The Cabinet-Maker and Upholsterer's Drawing Book.* Introduction by Joseph Aronson. Reprint of various early eds., 1793–1802. New York: Dover Publications, 1972.

Shoeser, Mary, and Celia Rufy. *English and American Textiles.* London: Thames and Hudson, 1989.

Snodin, Michael. *Karl Friederich Schinkel: A Universal Man.* New Haven and London: Yale University Press in association with the Victoria and Albert Museum, 1991.

Thornton, Peter. *Authentic Decor: The Domestic Interior, 1620–1920.* New York: Viking, 1984.

———. "French Beds." *Apollo,* March 1974, pp. 182–185.

———. *The Italian Renaissance Interior, 1400–1600.* London: Weidenfeld and Nicolson, 1991.

———. *Seventeenth-Century Interior Decoration in England, France and Holland.* New Haven and London: Yale University Press, 1978.

Von Furstenberg, Diane. *Beds.* New York: Bantam Books, 1991.

Vreeland, Diana. George Plimpton, ed. *D.V.* New York: Alfred A. Knopf, 1984.

Ward-Jackson, Peter. *English Furniture Designs of the Eighteenth Century.* London: Victoria and Albert Museum, 1984.

Watkins, Susan. *Jane Austen's Town and Country Style.* London: Thames and Hudson, 1990; New York: Rizzoli, 1990.

White, Elizabeth. *Pictorial Dictionary of British Eighteenth-Century Furniture Design.* Woodbridge, Suffolk, England: Antique Collectors Club, 1990.

Wright, Lawrence. *Warm and Snug: The History of the Bed.* London: Routledge and Kegan Paul, Ltd., 1962.

SHOPPING GUIDES

Brabec, Dominique and Eglé Salvy. *Paris Chic: The Parisian's Own Insider Shopping Guide.* London: Thames and Hudson, 1993.

Coté Sud. *Nos Bonnes Addresses 94–95.*

Gershman, Suzy. *Born to Shop: Italy.* New York: HarperCollins, 1993.

ACKNOWLEDGMENTS

I would like to express my sincerest thanks to everyone who contributed to this project in both large and small ways. I would especially like to thank all those at Abbeville whose enthusiastic participation has shaped this series: extra special thanks to my editor, Jacqueline Decter, with whom I have enjoyed working enormously, for her extraordinary dedication, commitment, and inspiration as well as her imaginative and insightful editing; Mark Magowan for his vision and unflagging support; designer Molly Shields for her creation of a superb visual presentation; Jennifer Pierson; Amy Metsch; Laura Straus; Paula Trotto; Myrna Smoot; and everyone behind the scenes whom I may not have met but whose involvement helped make this book a reality. I would also like to thank Marike Gauthier, Francine Sanllorente, and the staff at Editions Abbeville, Paris; John Murray, Stephanie Allen, Nicholas Perrin, and the staff at John Murray for their efforts on my behalf; Fritz von der Schulenburg for his superb photographs and "interior vision"; Karen Howes of The Interior World, not only for providing caption information and attributions but also for her friendship and support.

Special thanks to Alessandra Costamagna, Linda Costamagna, Lisa Eastman, Isabella Invernizzi, and Susan Tinsley for sharing their inveterate shopping expertise and for their help in preparing the list of sources; Anne Hardy of House & Garden, who is always full of ideas, suggestions, and friendship; Min Hogg, editor in chief of The World of Interiors, for kindly allowing me a glimpse of the magazine's archive as I embarked on this series.

To Trudi Ballard, Roger Banks-Pye, Ann Grafton, and Tom Parr at Colefax and Fowler for their help with this project, as well as to David Green and the Directors for hosting the splendid launch of The Dining Room, the first book in the series.

I would also like to thank the Chanel Boutique (Bond Street, London), Country Road, Patrick Cox Shoes, Frette, Pierre Frey, Judy Greenwood Antiques, Anya Hindmarch and Annabel Broadley of Anya Hindmarch, Pratesi, and Christine Halabi of Le Tissus Français.

In addition, I would like to thank Judith Elsdon, Sheila Little, and William McNaught of the American Museum in Britain; Serena and Julian Barrow; André de Cacqueray; Nina Campbell; François Valcke and Rupert Cavendish of Rupert Cavendish; Christopher Gibbs; Mark Weaver of Guinevere Antiques; Nicholas Haslam; Stephanie Hoppen; Tessa Kennedy; Baldassare La Rizza; Stefanie Maison; Isabelle King and David Mlinaric of Mlinaric, Henry and Zervudachi, Ltd.; Gail and William Monaghan; Judy Nyquist; Mimmi O'Connell; Carolyn Quartermaine; Sally Metcalfe of George Spencer; Stickland Coombe Architecture; Peter Thornton; Charlotte Heneage and Joanna Wood of Joanna Wood; Carinthia West; and Stephen Woodhams.

INDEX